COLLEGE STUDENT SUCCESS

James A. Bazán, MA
Laura L. Bazán, MS
Linda J. Dunham, MPH
Elvira D. Johnson, MA

4th edition 2012

Published by CPCC Press
PO Box 35009
Charlotte, NC 28235
cpccpress@cpcc.edu

Cover design by CPCC Community Relations & Marketing Services
ISBN: 978-1-59494-056-9

Published and Printed in the United States of America

For additional information, you are invited to contact:

Laura Bazán
Central Piedmont Community College
P.O. Box 35009
Charlotte, N.C. 28235-5009

Tel: 704.330.6417
E-mail: laura.bazan@cpcc.edu
Website: www.cpcc.edu
            www.cpccpress.com

CPCC Press is a division of Central Piedmont Community College Services Corporation.

Table of Contents

How To Use This Textbook

This textbook has been developed especially to support you as you become a college student. Used as part of a curriculum for student success courses, this book will guide you as you walk through the doors of college for the first (or second or third) time. Regardless of whether this is your first experience in college or you are returning or trying to get re-established in a post-secondary education, the information in this book will help you steer your way through unfamiliar territory.

Use this textbook as a resource. Consider it your personal set of directions for the next few semesters until you are completely situated in the culture of your college community.

Depending on the type of learner you are (you will learn more about this later in this textbook), you may want to think of it like this:

1. This textbook is the journal for your next few years. Write down everything in it that you need to remember about how to be successful.

2. This textbook will help you develop the map you will use to plot your journey. It will show you how to avoid making common errors in thinking which can lead to a longer and more expensive route to success.

3. This textbook lets you account for assets and liabilities that help you determine whether you are spending academic money and energy wisely.

4. This textbook is like the supervisor in your future career. You can decide not to follow the advice, but it might help you stick around.

Acknowledgments

This textbook is a collaboration of work done by many students, instructors, administrators, and resource personnel.

If it were not for students like you who come to college in search of an enriched life through education, there would be no need for this textbook. Because of those students, the authors were able to identify a community of resources that facilitate successful learning.

This community of resources includes people as well as areas. It is important to acknowledge the personal and individual commitment to education that is offered by all personnel at any institution of higher learning. From the facility and staff to the President's office, the dedication and obligation to help students in their educational endeavors is commendable.

We believe that the fundamental commitment to success evident in the collaborative efforts of the college administrators, students, writers, teachers, broadcast specialists, production managers, counselors, advisors, resource personnel, and administrative assistants who made this textbook possible is what enables students to realize their goals with innovation and integrity.

We thank each of you for your contributions.

James A. Bazán, MA
Laura L. Bazán, MS
Linda J. Dunham, MPI
Elvira D. Johnson, M/

Introduction to the Textbook

Systems run nearly everything we do in schools and business. We even have systems in place in our homes that keep track of our spending, tell us when doors and windows are opened, and monitor the temperature levels for our comfort.

It is natural and necessary for systems to operate colleges, but the truth is that the systems are run by *people*. The purpose of this textbook is to provide a comfortable, safe space for students to learn about the systems that can help them succeed in college.

This textbook was written with people in mind. It orients students to themselves and to college in general. In it, you will answer some very important questions such as:

> - What kind of person are you?
> - How did you get where you are academically?
> - What kind of learner are you?
> - Why are you in college?
> - What are your academic goals?
> - How do you plan to reach your goals?
> - What is going on in the world that aligns with your academic goals?

You will interact with technology and learn about your college's resources in addition to setting some clear goals for your future.

We know that learning does not stop when you finish this textbook. This textbook will help you develop, expand and continue your educational journey. Students are engaged in an academic path that will change their lives. We hope this textbook helps you chart your course through that adventure.

Brief Description of College Student Success

What is the meaning of success? Most people answer that question by asking more questions. Success in what? Success for whom? It is almost as if we have to qualify the type and significance of success as it relates to the individual pursuing it.

That may be exactly correct. "Success" may be the most individual and relative term in the world. For the person who is hungry, success may be being able to find food for the day. For the person who is trying to land that million dollar client, success may be a productive conversation at a lunch meeting. For the unmarried mother of two children who is struggling to finish the semester at community college, success may be finishing four classes toward her major.

In writing this textbook, the term became more elusive than ever. We, the authors, found that there are as many ways to define success as there are ways to be successful. We hope that you will find your own definition of college student success as you move closer to your goal. Success is an elusive thing – the closer we get to what we think success may be, the more it becomes something else. It may become richer, deeper and more complicated or it may become simpler and more defined. Whichever way your college student success evolves, it is a good idea to be aware of what is happening.

This textbook serves as a platform from which students can make decisions about the pathways and processes that are integral to their personal college student success.

There is no right way to success. There is no wrong way to success. The way you choose is successful if you are happy with the outcome.

Goals of this Textbook:

- To introduce the basics of college life and provide students with skills to function effectively in the college environment.

- To provide a general orientation to college and various departments vital to student success.

- To begin the self-assessment process necessary to develop a strategic academic plan for college success.

- To learn the skills involved in setting goals and developing an action plan through objectives.

- To learn basic study skills necessary for academic success.

UNIT 1
IT'S ABOUT YOU

Unit 1: It's About You

Who do you think you are? How many times (and ways) have you heard that question asked? But who do you think you are? We all have thoughts, or glimpses, of who we are, but never a clear or complete picture.

Relax. It is perfectly normal to be a work in progress. The truth is that the "work in progress" may take your whole life. Change is the most dependable thing in life. Not only will your needs, dreams, and plans change, but even your ideas about these things will change.

At one time, people with a high school diploma in the United States could make a good living working in a factory or a trade. The "American dream" did not require a college education. Now, however, 60 percent of all jobs require some education beyond the high school level. In 1956, in another example, the median age at first marriage for women was 20.1—half of the women who were married for the first time were younger than 20.1. People planned to marry immediately after high school. By 2009, that median age had increased to 26.5. (US Census 2011) Now, even women who plan to marry can expect to finish college and get started on their career before getting married. These larger social changes alter the way people plan their lives.

Adjusting to change is an often misunderstood aspect of getting a college education. There have always been nay-sayers who dismiss the "self-discovery" aspect of education. A recent Pew Research Center poll found that 57 percent of respondents said that college failed to provide good value for the money, and 75 percent said it was too expensive for the average person to afford. Astonishingly, though, 86 percent of recent graduates described college as a good investment for themselves (Pew, 2011). Maybe those recent graduates have seen that the discovery process required by education has far-reaching effects. The process of letting go of an old idea to "discover" a new idea in math, for example, is the same as the process of deciding what major to select. The process of taking responsibility for getting work done is the same process required to address grievances. All of that requires learning how to manage and deal with change.

It is because of those sorts of changes that you are here. College is all about change. Dissatisfaction with the way things are, or have always been, is what makes us initiate a new focus for our lives. Once you set the wheels in motion for a college education you discover that this is a lot different from anything you have ever known.

You have decided that you want to be in college. This may have been a scary decision. You may be testing the waters or already dedicated to an educational plan that takes you from this course through a degree program and on to further education. Whatever your goals may be, you can be confident that the material in this course is designed with you in mind. It will introduce some of the people at your college who have a sincere interest in your educational success. We want you to have the skills and resources necessary to follow your dream.

This unit will help you discover aspects of yourself that you may have suspected, aspects that you may have been told you had, and some you may already know. Some discoveries may offer completely new insights. In any case, you can enhance these understandings by digging deeply into the material and becoming involved in your college community.

Teams of experts created the Learning Style Assessment and Personality Inventory specifically to address the needs of students. You will use the results of these assessments to learn to create an educational action plan for your academic career.

These assessments will never give you a complete picture of who you are. They will, however, offer insights, options, and alternative ways of looking at yourself to help you become successful in your academic pursuits.

Getting Started:

The following pages include some first-day activities for getting oriented to your college environment, your classmates and to your instructor. It's effective for you to become acquainted with others when you start classes, but it can make students feel awkward and uncomfortable.

In his textbook, *Becoming a Master Student* (2011) Dave Ellis talks about a Power Process called "Risk Being a Fool" as a way to mastery, not mediocrity.

Risk being a fool means that foolishness-along with courage, cowardice, grace, and clumsiness-is a human characteristic. We all share it. ...There is one sure-fire way to avoid any risk of being a fool, and that's to avoid life. The writer who never finishes a book will never have to worry about getting negative reviews. The center fielder who sits out every game is safe from making any errors. And the comedian who never performs in front of an audience is certain to avoid telling jokes that fall flat. The possibility of succeeding at any venture increases when we're comfortable with making mistakes – that is, with the risk of being a fool" (Ellis, D., 2011).

The activities on the following pages will help you take a look at where you are right now in the process of thinking about your goals and academic career.

First-Day Activities

Student Profile Sheet

Complete the following to provide a more complete picture of yourself as a student.

Name	
E-mail address	
Phone number	
Where/when I attended high school	
My hobbies are	
I am really good at	
My favorite kind of music is	
One person I would love to meet is	
My favorite kind of food is	
My favorite childhood memory is	
People usually think that I am	
If I could have anything I wanted	
1 thing I would change about the world	
One thing that I have learned in life is	
If I could live anywhere I wanted	
I am here because	
My 3 worst fears about college are	
The kind of student I am is	
I am taking this class because	
What I want to learn in this class is/are	
I want the instructor to know	
I want to know about the instructor	

Meet Your Classmates

Introduce yourself to the other students in your class by greeting each of them with a warm smile and a professional handshake. Select a question from this sheet and ask that person. If someone can answer yes, then ask that person to sign your sheet. He or she can then ask you a question and get your signature. Continue until you have completed the sheet.

1. Who is proficient at using a computer?   _____

2. Who has worked in a restaurant?   _____

3. Who has dated someone longer than a year?   _____

4. Who can balance a checkbook?   _____

5. Who ate breakfast this morning?   _____

6. Who likes to work with plants?   _____

7. Who loves math?   _____

8. Who is creative?   _____

9. Who can change a tire?   _____

10. Who wants to own his/her own business?   _____

11. Who can speak another language?   _____

12. Who is a very positive person?   _____

13. Who has read a book this month?   _____

14. Who is a good decorator?   _____

15. Who can play a musical instrument?   _____

Evaluating Your Academic Behavior

Check off the following academic behaviors according to what you currently do, what you will start to do, and what you think won't work. Evaluate why you think certain behaviors will not work. Are these behaviors essential to success? Why or why not?

I do this	I will start	It won't work	Behavior
			Attend every class
			Come to every class on time
			Be alert and attentive in class
			Ask at least one question during class
			Show interest in the discussion
			Ask when I don't understand
			Get outside tutoring
			Have someone proofread all my papers
			Set up a meeting with the instructor
			E-mail the instructor if I miss a class
			Get to know the instructor
			Show respect for the instructor
			Show respect for fellow classmates
			Set goals and objectives for classes
			Evaluate myself in each class
			Keep a grade sheet in each class
			Make at least one new friend per class
			Have a positive attitude

The Course Syllabus

Understanding and knowing how to use the course syllabus is integral to being successful in college. The course syllabus will tell you what will be expected of you during the term, the course requirements, how to get in touch with your instructor, and policies on absences and missed work.

Work in pairs or in groups to answer the following questions about your course syllabus.

Introduction and Instructor Information:

1. What is the name and contact information for your instructor? What is the best way to reach him/her?

2. What important dates are necessary to know to be successful in this course?

3. What materials are required for this course? What materials are recommended?

4. What are the course objectives? What is it you will be expected to know by the end of the term?

Student Responsibilities:

5. What is the attendance policy for the course?

6. What is the make-up policy for work missed?

7. What is the grading policy for the course? How will your grade be calculated?

8. Where will your cumulative grade be kept? Online? With the instructor? With you? How can you keep up with your grades?

9. What are the major assignments for the course?

10. How many quizzes? Will there be a mid-term? Final exam?

Other information important for success in this class:

SYLLABUS ACTIVITY

Complete the following grid below to have a visual display of your courses and requirements for the term.

Course	Section	Class Time	Instructor Info	Textbook Materials	Drop/Add Date	Withdrawal Date	Attendance Info	Make-Up Work	Assign ments	Quizzes (#,dates)	Mid-Term	Final Exam

Names and Numbers of Classmates:

Learning Styles and Personality Types

Have you noticed that some students seem to be able to do all the right things when it comes to being a traditional college student? They go to class, take impeccable notes, read complex textbook material and get good grades without, seemingly, losing sleep or tearing their hair out before exams. How do they do that? Perhaps it is because their study skills match their learning style, and they have discovered the best way for them to learn information.

What are Learning Styles, and why should you learn about them?

How do you learn best? How much do you really know about your learning style? In which classes do you have a difficult time understanding the material? Why? Often, it is because we do not really know the best way for us to learn.

Learning styles refer to your preferred ways to perceive and process new information. Perceiving refers to how you take in information, and processing refers to how you organize the information and make it meaningful.

Suppose you have just purchased a new cell phone. How will you learn to navigate the phone's features and tools? Will you read the instructions, ask friends to show you how to use it, or just try out the different settings and features until you figure it out on your own? Maybe you will take all of those approaches to learning, but one of them will feel more natural to you.

Think of a class in which you had difficulty learning because the material was new to you. If you've never taken a business law class, the course content will be foreign to you. Will you read the textbook, ask a friend to explain it to you, just sit in class and listen, or try a variety of techniques to help you learn the material? Learning new course content is similar to learning how to operate a new piece of technology. The more you know about the way you learn, the easier it will be to apply those learning strategies to your courses.

Self-Assessments

What is the secret to success in college? There is no secret, but there are plenty of tools and strategies to assist you in becoming successful. One such tool is a learning style assessment. This tool can help you discover your learning style. It provides a key to the ways you perceive and process new information.

Self-assessments will help you determine some of the most effective ways you learn. Some of those ways have been defined as Visual, Auditory, and Kinesthetic, while others delve deeply into the characteristics and causes for your behavior. Whichever type of assessment you use, it is important to know that lives are changeable, but tendencies are somewhat ingrained. It is those tendencies toward certain preferences and behaviors that will help you see what works for you and what does not.

You might be asking: "Why should I take learning styles assessment? I already know how I learn." The way we think we learn may be the result of bad habits or misinformation. Do you know someone who thinks they can sing but seems to be a victim of misinformation about his or her talents? Good voice teachers argue they can teach anyone to sing, and. singing well is often a practice of developing good habits. The results of your learning styles assessment can provide you with valuable information to help you develop good study skills and to help you understand the teaching styles of your college instructors.

Can knowledge of my Learning Styles really help me to improve my grades?

Students who incorporate their learning style into their study skill may feel more confident in their abilities and may be more productive because they are using a method of learning that is comfortable for them (Gross Davis, 1977).

Sometimes the instructor will not teach in the style that matches your learning style. Knowing how to adapt what you receive into your preferred learning styles will make learning more efficient. Being flexible in your learning style – allowing yourself to learn with a combination of visual, auditory, and kinesthetic/tactile methods – will enhance your ability to absorb material from a variety of techniques and strategies.

Remember, the way you process information is unique to you. If you discover how you process information, you can become more efficient when learning in class or studying for exams. Once you understand how you learn, you may feel more confident in your abilities to learn new information. Students who become comfortable with their style of learning will be better prepared to try out new and different styles of learning. Watch how you use your style as you make your way through the challenges of college.

Student Voices: LaTonya

LaTonya never understood why she earned "A"s in her math classes, but struggled to receive "C's" in her history and psychology classes. She had difficulty understanding those courses. She always thought it was her fault that she didn't understand history and psychology concepts. Once she completed a learning style inventory, she found that she had a strong preference for visual learning. LaTonya discovered she needed to see material to understand it. Now it all made sense to her. The math classes were taught visually: problems and computation on the board and practice work in notebooks. Her history class was lecture based, with very few visual cues used to support the lecture. After reading about ways to enhance her other learning styles, LaTonya found it helpful to read the chapters in her history textbook prior to attending the lectures. She also found brief video clips of topics covered in her history class to help her visualize the content.

Your Voice:

1. Why did LaTonya have difficulty with the material in some of her courses?

2. What teaching methods do most instructors use?

3. Is your learning style reflected in the courses in which you have difficulty?

4. How can you use your learning style to improve your performance in courses in which you have difficulty?

Learning Styles Characteristics and Tips

Learning Style	Characteristics	Learning Tips
Visual	• Needs to see it to know it • Has strong sense of color • May have artistic ability • Has difficulty with spoken directions • Is easily distracted by sounds • Has trouble following lectures • Misinterprets spoken words	• Use graphics to reinforce • Use color coding to organize notes and possessions • Use written directions • Use flow charts and diagrams for note-taking • Visualize spelling of words • Recopy class notes during study time
Auditory	• Prefers to get information by listening • Needs to hear or speak it to know it • Has trouble following written directions • Prefers listening over reading and writing • Is frequently unable to read body language	• Use tapes when reading and taking class lecture notes • Learn by interviewing or participating in discussions • Work in study groups • Read test questions out loud or put on tape • Recite information that is important to remember
Kinesthetic	• Prefers hands-on learning • Can assemble parts without reading directions • Has difficulty sitting still • Learns better with physical activity • May be well coordinated with athletic ability	• Learn experientially (making models, doing lab work, etc) • Take frequent breaks during study periods • Trace letters while spelling • Use a computer to reinforce learning • Memorize while pacing or exercising • Bring some type of "grip toy" to class to hold

List of

Strategies to Enhance Your Learning Style

Learning Style Strategies

Try some of these techniques in the next few days to help enhance your learning style. Add your own strategies for use at work and at home.

If you are a Kinesthetic learner or wish to enhance this learning style:

At School:

1. Rewrite your class notes later the same day. The act of moving your hand as you write will help you remember your material.
2. Get your body involved in as much movement as possible while you study.
3. Take walks during study breaks (as often as every fifteen minutes). As you walk, think about what you are studying.
4. Choose classes that allow you to participate in tasks. You will learn much more when you are a part of a demonstration or lab activity.
5. Bring a grip toy to class (rubber ball, unusual pen, or something to squeeze). Squeezing the object will help keep you from getting bored and will satisfy your need to get up and move around.
6. With your finger, trace words in the air or on your desk while you are spelling them.
7. When memorizing facts, write them down several times.
8. Use the computer to reinforce learning by accessing companion websites.
9. Form a study group.
10. Sit in the front of the class to minimize distractions

Add some techniques for work and home that would support the kinesthetic learner:

At Work:

At Home:

If you are a Visual learner or wish to enhance this learning style:

At School:

1. Take notes in class.
2. While reading, write notes about the main idea of each paragraph. You only need to write one or two words that will remind you what the paragraph is about.
3. Pay special attention to the pictures in your textbook and the writing next to the pictures.
4. Create mental pictures that illustrate analytical or logical concepts.
5. Write on index cards important ideas that need review. Visual learners benefit greatly from this technique.
6. Use large poster boards to organize information and processes.
7. Use color to categorize and memorize different topics.
8. Use a variety of note taking methods such as Cornell, mind-maps, and outlines.
9. Use varied fonts and styles when re-typing notes to help you differentiate change.
10. Use pictures and symbols to accompany topics when taking notes.

Add some strategies for work and home that would support the visual learner:

At Work:

At Home:

If you are an Auditory learner or wish to enhance this learning style:

At School:

1. Read aloud. It will help with your concentration.

2. Make a special effort to always take notes

3. Form study groups with your friends and classmates and talk about the material you are learning.

4. Read your notes, ideas, and questions into a tape recorder and listen to the tape as you study.

5. Tape record your class lectures and listen to the lectures again. Write additional notes while listening to lectures.

6. Tape record verbal summaries of relevant reading.

7. Participate in oral discussions of written material.

8. Learn to spell by repeating the letters out loud.

9. Use sound and word association for note memorization.

10. Ask questions and engage in classroom conversation.

Add some strategies for work and home that would support the auditory learner:

At Work:

At Home:

Personality Types

How does your personality affect the way you learn? How does your instructor's personality affect the way he or she teaches?

Taking a personality type assessment can help you recognize your preferences, your likely responses, and your behavior. But can an assessment predict success? It can no more predict success than it can excuse bad habits or behavior. What students *can* do with their personality type assessment is identify patterns of likely behaviors in their day-to-day activities. Is there a reason why some students have particularly organized notebooks and planners while others seem to thrive on chaos? Why do some go with their "gut" feelings while others need facts to decide?

In education, as in love and at work, we react and respond to our environment and to people in varied ways. The important thing to keep in mind is that by looking at ourselves we're more likely to understand some of the reasons *why* we do the things we do. Keep an open mind. Ask questions. Do not be afraid to take an honest look at your life. This will help to broaden our depth and scope of insight.

The purpose of this part of the textbook is to help you identify some of the reasons why you do the things you do. If you are interested in changing some of your behaviors, this inventory can give you some insights about boosting those areas in which you are doing well and improving behaviors that may not be working for you as well as you would like. You may be able to better understand the personalities of your instructors and classmates by reading some of the information available.

Sample Personality Types

Your instructor may require you to take a personality inventory as part of this course. Often, these inventories report results in categories such as: **E**xtrovert – **I**ntrovert – **S**ensing – **I**ntuitive; **T**hinking – **F**eeling; and **J**udging – **P**erceiving.

The groupings below represent careers and jobs people of various personality types enjoy doing. It is important to remember that these do not list all the jobs possible under each heading. Even more importantly – people can and do fill jobs dissimilar to their personality, and it sometimes works out quite well. Use these groupings as a tool for getting new ideas about careers and jobs you might enjoy.

ISTJ
Management, Accounting, Auditing, Efficiency Expert, Geologist, Bank Examiner, Organizational Development, Electrician, Dentist, Pharmacist, School Principal, School bus Driver, File Clerk, Stock Broker, Legal Secretary, Computer Operator, Computer Programmer, Technical Writer, Chief Information Officer, Police Officer, Real Estate Agent

ISFJ
Ministry, Library Work, Nursing, Secretary, Curator, Bookkeeper, Dental Hygienist, Computer Operator, Personnel Administrator, Paralegal, Real Estate Agent, Artist, Interior Decorator, Retail Owner, Musician, Elementary Teacher, Physical Therapist, Nurse, Social Worker, Personnel Counselor, Alcohol/Drug Counselor

ISTP
Surveyor, Fire Fighter, Private Investigator, Pilot or Police Officer, Purchasing Agent, Chiropractor, Medical Technician, Securities Analyst, Computer Repair Person, Race Car Driver, Computer Programmer, Electrical Engineer, Legal Secretary, Coach/Trainer, Commercial Artist, Carpenter, Paralegal, Dental Assistant, Radiological Technician, Marine Biologist, Software Developer

ISFP
Bookkeeper, Clerical, Dental Assistant, Physical Therapist, Mechanic, Radiology Technologist, Surveyor, Chef, Forester, Geologist, Landscaper/Designer, Crisis Hotline Operator, Elementary Teacher, Beautician, Typist, Jeweler, Gardener, Potter or Painter, Botanist, Marine Biologist, Social Worker

INFJ
Career Counselor, Psychologist, Educational Consultant, Teacher: Special Education, Librarian, Artist, Playwright, Novelist/Poet Editor/Art Director, Graphic Designer, HR Manager, Merchandise Planner, Environmental Lawyer, Marketer, Job Analyst, Mental Health Counselor, Dietician/Nutritionist, Research, Educational Consultant, Architect, Interpreter/Translator

INTJ
Management, Consultant, Economist, Scientist, Computer Programmer, Environmental Planner, New Business Developer, Curriculum Designer, Administrator, Mathematician, Psychologist, Neurologist, Biomedical Researcher, Strategic Planner, Civil Engineer, Intellectual Properties Attorney, Designer, Editor/Art Director, Inventor, Graphic Designer, Financial Planner, Judge

INFP
Information-Graphic Designer, College Professor, Researcher, Legal Mediator, Social Worker, Holistic Health Practitioner, Occupational Therapist, Diversity Manager, Human Resources, Employment Development Specialist, Minister/Priest/Rabbi Missionary, Psychologist, Writer: Poet/Novelist Journalist, Editor/Art Director, Organization Development Specialist

INTP
Strategic Planner, Writer, Staff Development, Lawyer, Architect, Software Designer, Financial Analyst, College Professor, Photographer, Logician, Artist, Systems Analyst, Neurologist, Physicist, Psychologist, Research/Development, Computer Programmer, Data Base Manager, Chemist, Biologist, Investigator

ESTP
Real Estate Broker, Chef, Land Developer, Physical Therapist, Stock Broker, News Reporter, Fire Fighter, Promoter, Entrepreneur, Pilot, Budget Analyst, Insurance Agent, Management Consultant, Franchise Owner, Electrical Engineer, Aircraft Mechanic, Technical Trainer, EEG Technician, Radiological Technician, Emergency Medical Technician, Corrections Officer, Flight Attendant

ESFP
Veterinarian, Flight Attendant, Floral Designer, Real Estate Agent, Child Care Provider, Social Worker, Fundraiser, Athletic Coach, Musician, Secretary, Receptionist, Special Events Producer, Teacher: Preschool, Teacher: Elementary, Emergency Room Nurse, Occupational Therapist, Exercise Physiologist, Team Trainer, Travel, Sales, Public Relations Specialist, Waiter/Waitress, Labor Relations, Mediator

ESTJ
Government Employee, Pharmaceutical Sales, Auditor, Computer Analyst, Technical Trainer, Project Manager ,Office Manager, Factory Supervisor, Credit Analyst, Electrical Engineer, Stockbroker, Regulatory Compliance Officer, Chief Information Officer, Construction Worker, General Contractor, Paralegal, Industrial Engineer, Budget Analyst, Database Manager, Funeral Director, Cook, Security Guard, Dentist

ESFJ
Nurse, Social Worker, Caterer, Flight Attendant, Bookkeeper, Medical/Dental Assistant, Exercise Physiologist, Elementary Teacher, Minister/Priest/Rabbi, Retail Owner, Office Manager, Telemarketer, Counselor, Teacher: Special Education, Merchandise Planner, Credit Counselor, Athletic Coach, Insurance Agent, Sales Representative, Massage Therapist, Medical Secretary, Child Care Provider, ESL Teacher

ENFP
Conference Planner, Speech Pathologist, HR Development/Trainer, Ombudsman, Clergy, Journalist, Newscaster, Career Counselor, Housing Director, Character Actor, Marketing

Consultant, Musician/Composer, Artist, Information-Graphic Designer, HR Manager, Merchandise Planner, Advertising Manager, Dietician/Nutritionist, Massage Therapist, Editor/Art Director

ENTP

Venture Capitalist, Actor, Journalist, Investment Broker, Real Estate Agent, Real Estate Developer, Strategic Planner, Political Manager, Politician, Special Projects Developer, Literary Agent, Restaurant/Bar Owner, Technical Trainer, Diversity Manager, Art Director, Personnel, Systems Developer, Computer Analyst, Logistics, Consultant, Advertising, Creative Director, Radio/TV Talk Show Host

ENFJ

Entertainer, Recruiter, Artist, Newscaster, Writer/Journalist, Recreation Director, Librarian, Facilitator, Politician, Psychologist, Housing Director, Career Counselor, Sales Trainer, Travel Agent, Program Designer, Corporate Trainer, Child Welfare Worker, Social Worker (Elder Services), Interpreter/Translator, Occupational Therapist, Executive: Small Business, Alcohol/Drug Counselor, Sales Manager

ENTJ

Program Designer, Attorney, Administrator, Officer, Manager, Chemical Engineer, Sales Manager, Logistics Consultant, Franchise Owner, New Business Developer, Personnel Manager, Investment Banker, Labor Relations, Management, Trainer, Credit Investigator, Mortgage Broker, Corporate Trainer, Environmental Engineer, Biomedical Engineer, Business Consultant, Educational Consultant, Personal Finance Planner, Network Integration Specialist, Media/Buyer Planner

(CPCC, 2012)

ACADEMIC HISTORY

A personal academic history does not begin with you. It begins with the academic history of the people who raised you to adulthood.

What is the academic history of your nuclear family? Did they finish high school? Are you from a long line of high school and college graduates or are you the first person to finish high school and go to college? All of these sociological and psychological contexts help shape the feelings, beliefs, and attitudes that you have about high education.

Take a moment to look over Carlos' Educational Genealogy and then fill out the chart included with your information. Discuss your chart with your classmates.

Student Voices: Carlos

Carlos wants to be a nurse. He grew up in a family of healthcare providers. Both of his parents are healthcare professionals. His father is a pediatrician and his mother is a medical assistant at a health clinic. In high school, Carlos was a C student, but got A's in his science classes. Over the years, Carlos has seen first-hand the importance of providing healthcare to the community. His desire to help others and to follow in his parents' footsteps has motivated him to look into careers in the healthcare field. The career path to become a physician was too long, so Carlos plans to complete a degree in nursing. His high school grades kept him from attending a four year school, so he has been working until he can decide what to do. He has several options. He can enroll at the community  college, complete his associate's degree and transfer to a university to complete his BS in nursing, or he can apply directly to the local hospital's nursing school program. The community college option works well with his financial situation and his work schedule.

Your Voice:

1. Why does Carlos believe that choosing a nursing degree is the right career path for him?

2. What influence does Carlos' academic history have on the choices he is making?

3. What part of your academic history influences you positively or negatively in your academic path?

Educational Genealogy - CARLOS

Relationship	Earlier	1950s	1960s	1970s	1980s	1990s	2000s	2010s	2020s	2030s
Mother Justina			Immigrated to US from Guatemala		Graduated HS	Medical Assistant Degree from CC	Working in health clinic	Lead Assistant at Medical Clinic		
Father Joaquin			Immigrated to US from Guatemala	Graduated HS, Graduated College	Med School, Internship	Medical Residency and Practice	Practicing Pediatric Medicine	Partner in Pediatric Medicine Practice		
Brother Jose							Graduated HS	Attending CC		
Brother Juan						Graduated HS	Works at a restaurant			
Sister Anita							Graduated HS	Attending College		
Grandmother Josephina		Graduated HS in Mexico	Immigrated to US from Guatemala	Attended ESL classes	Work as translator for DSS.	↑	↑			
Grandfather Martin		Attended HS in Mexico, did not graduate	Immigrated to US from Guatemala	Attended ESL classes. Attended CC HS & AA in Engineering	Work as foreman at nuclear power plant	↑	↑			
Uncle Ruben		Attended school to grade 7	Living and working as tailor in Guatemala	↑	↑					
Friend/Teammate Trey							Graduated HS	Enrolled in State University		

Page | 35

Your Educational Genealogy:

Now it's your turn. It is helpful to see the trends and patterns of education in friends and families. Fill out the chart below with information from *your* family's educational history. To do this, you may have to conduct some interviews with family members. Start with the people in your immediate family and then branch out to grandparents, great-grandparents, distant aunts, uncles, cousins from all parts of your family tree. Include friends or acquaintances that have influenced your education.

When you have done a thorough job of recording this information, answer the questions on the next page:

Educational Genealogy

Relationship	Earlier	1950s	1960s	1970s	1980s	1990s	2000s	2010s	2020s	2030s

Educational Genealogy Questions:

1. Where do you find yourself in the educational history of your family?

2. What made you decide to attend college?

3. Who on your chart has most influenced or motivated you (positively or negatively) to continue your education?

4. Write a statement about how your friends and family have influenced your educational needs, dreams, plans and ideas.

Why College?

There are probably as many reasons to not go to college as there are reasons to go. The big question is: why did *you* decide to go to college?

Here are some common reasons why people decide to get education past high school. How many of them match yours?

- [ ] It's the only way to pursue my chosen career.
- [ ] Because I'm not sure what I want to do, so I want to experience college to find out.
- [ ] My job situation has changed. I need to upgrade my education.
- [ ] My parents want me to go.
- [ ] All of my friends are going and I don't want to be left behind.
- [ ] I'm looking for a boyfriend/girlfriend/wife/husband/partner
- [ ] I want to earn more money.
- [ ] I need to get out of my parents' house.
- [ ] I want to get out of my town.
- [ ] I had a teacher in high school that encouraged me to go to college.
- [ ] I got a scholarship.
- [ ] I got a loan.
- [ ] My family has been saving money for my college education.
- [ ] I want to improve my life.
- [ ] I love to party.

Here are some common reasons why people decide to NOT get education past high school. How many of them match yours?

- [ ] No one in my family has ever gone to college. They'll tease me.
- [ ] I'll be losing 4-5 working years.
- [ ] I don't need to be in a classroom to learn how to do a job.
- [ ] Plenty of other people did just fine without going to college (my rich uncle, Bill Gates, Michael Dell, Quentin Tarantino, Henry Ford, and Thomas Edison).
- [ ] I'm doing well in my job now. I don't need a degree.
- [ ] I don't have enough money to go to college.
- [ ] I don't think I'm smart enough to go to college.
- [ ] I won't fit in.
- [ ] I'm too old.
- [ ] I didn't do very well in high school.
- [ ] College is too hard.
- [ ] I got in trouble with the law and have a "record." They probably won't let me in.
- [ ] I'm undocumented.
- [ ] I have children - it's too much to work, take care of a family and go to school.
- [ ] I don't have any computer skills, don't have internet access or own a computer.
- [ ] It's been too long since I was in high school. It would be like starting over with much younger classmates.
- [ ] I don't know anyone who goes to college. I would be completely on my own.

Personal Narrative

Write a personal narrative explaining why you are in college and what you want to accomplish. You may want to give a brief history of the events that brought you here and what you plan to do once you finish this phase of your education.

Your personal narrative should be a full page narrative essay. It should address the following questions:

1. Why did you decide to attend college?

2. How does the Educational Genealogy of your family and friends affect your decision to attend college? What have you been told by these influential people about attending college? How has that affected your decision?

3. What circumstances determined your decision to attend *this* college? What other options were available to you?

4. What do you hope to accomplish by attending college?

5. What do you plan to do when you finish your work at this college?

_____

_____

_____

_____

_____

_____

_____

_____

_____

_____

_____

Now that you have spent some time thinking about why you decided to go to college, take a look at your expectations about what it means to go to college.

What is a Global Student?

An old joke asks and answers a series of questions:

"What do you call someone who speaks three languages?" Answer: "Trilingual." "Well, then, what do you call someone who speaks two languages?" Answer: "Bilingual." "And what do you call someone who speaks only one language?" Answer: "American."

Fortunately for the economy of the United States, that joke is not as valid as it was a few years ago. Increasingly, Americans are learning other languages. The ability to speak more than one language is an essential tool in operating in a global economy. If you are reading this text, you operate in a global economy. This textbook was printed by CPCC Press, a part of the Services Corporation operated by Central Piedmont Community College. CPCC is a large community college annually serving more than 70,000 members of the community in and around Charlotte, North Carolina. At any given time, it has students from more than 155 countries (CPCC, 2012). Many of those international students return to their countries of origin to work in their own local economies. Many others return home to work in international businesses. Still others are part of the largest wave of immigration in recent U.S. history.

But it is still true that many of us still operate in a self-imposed "filter bubble" when it comes to issues of global awareness. Have you ever noticed that some people disappear from your Facebook feed? Pariser (2011) uses the term "filter bubbles" to describe the filters created by

search-engine algorithms that screen the results when we use search engines such as Google, or news feeds such as Yahoo News, or shopping sites such as Amazon or Net-Flix. This is why Amazon and Netflix can make suggestions for you. In each of those sites, the options you see are based on many factors, such as your personal search histories, the specific location you are searching from, and other "markers". In some ways, we can think of limitations on global awareness as creating a

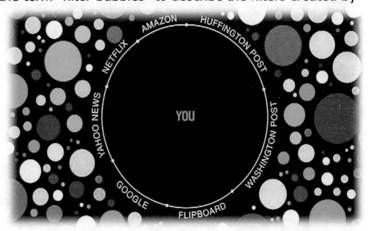

TED. 2011. "Beware Online Filter Bubbles."

"filter bubble". What we can learn is limited by what we have experienced, and too often we are not even aware that there are other options. There is nothing wrong with this—it is inevitable that we see what we are used to seeing, and that we are comfortable with what we already know.

You may be able to see some of your own filters—some of the expectations you bring to the "search engine" of your everyday life—by looking back at your educational genealogy. What aspects of your education brought you here? Why did you not end up somewhere else? Did you consider applying to Ulan Bator University? List a few of the reasons you did not apply for admission to UBU for further discussion see Global Awareness Filters on page 43.

A lot of times the idea of a "global economy" or a "multinational corporation" seems vague. It might help to remember that every one of us is embedded in that global economy. Sometimes the effect of globalization is obvious, as when you buy gasoline at a price influenced (in part) by a crisis a half a world away. We can pop the filter bubble by reflecting on that crisis and its effect on the price of gasoline. Sometimes the effect of globalization is fun. You pop the filter bubble when we try a new food at an ethnic restaurant. Other times, the effects of globalization are more subtle and more personal. An often overlooked aspect of globalization is represented by the diversity we have in our neighborhoods and our classrooms. As we see in Table 1, the United States population is approaching historical averages in the levels of foreign-born population. This means that we really do not have to look far to see the potential for and impact of global awareness.

Table 1

Foreign born as a percentage of the total US population

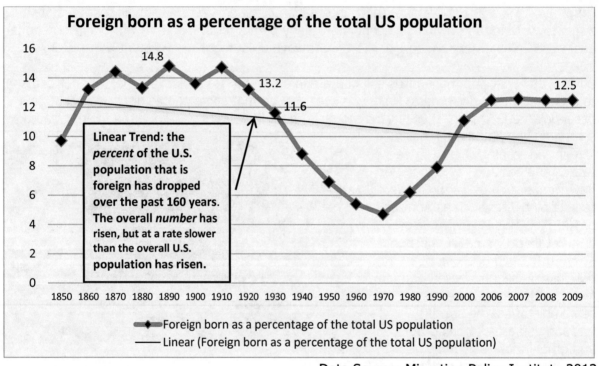

Data Source: Migration Policy Institute 2012

In raw numbers, the current population of "foreign born" in the United States is the largest in U.S. history. Since the last large wave of immigration at the beginning of the 20th Century, of course, the U.S. population has tripled. That means that the proportion of the population that is foreign born is not as large a *percentage* of the U.S. as it was between 1850 and 1930. This variation offers several lenses through which we can look at the issue of our global population.

Global Awareness filters:

1. Geographically, where did you go to school (if different places, list them)?

2. Geographically, where do you now go to school?

3. Compare and contrast answers 1 and 2. How did the similarities or differences shape your expectations?

4. Where were your friends from when you were growing up?

5. Where are most of your friends from now? List countries, regions.

6. Compare and contrast answers 4 and 5. How did the similarities or differences between you and them shape your expectations of your relationship?

7. From what religious background were most of your friends when you were growing up?

8. What religious background do most of your friends have now?

9. Compare and contrast answers 7 and 8. How did the similarities or differences between you and them shape your expectations of your relationship?

10. Why is it important to understand global awareness filters in your college career?

International context of school and community

Find out what you can about the makeup of your school. Get information about international students from the International Student Office, or its equivalent.

- To put that information in perspective, the U.S. Census Bureau has good data on numbers of people in your community who were born in other countries, and what countries they were born in. At the Census website, the information from the American Community Survey is generally the most accurate and most up-to-date.

- Another good source is the Migration Policy Institute, which offers fact sheets on U.S. immigration as well as a more global perspective on international migration.

- Cautionary note: there are many organizations that have particular pro- or anti-immigration agendas that have "official sounding" names. Doing a general web search for information on this topic will almost certainly result in unreliable information.

Family background
Where does your family come from?

- Sometimes we can illustrate that by asking where our family name comes from. Other times, as with many African Americans, our family names point to the very specific histories of very specific regions. This is important information. For example, a student in a large southeastern college knew his family was Gullah from the South Carolina Sea Islands. With a little searching, he was able to give a report on the rice culture of Sierra Leone and the development of the South Carolina economy.

- Are there any special foods that "mark" your family as coming from a distinctive region? For example, do you like livermush—a Southern regional food made of pig's liver, parts of the pig's head, and cornmeal and spices? In every class, there are several students who have never heard the words "liver" and "mush" put together as a marketing tool. Just as many light up at the idea of some good fried livermush for breakfast.

International education systems

You might want to put your college experience in a global perspective. How do educational systems and educational opportunities differ around the world? China, for example, has been radically expanding its universities. The number of students in colleges and universities grew 500 percent from 1999 to 2005 (Li, et al., 2008). Look at educational statistics from two or three countries and use that information to consider your own opportunities.

College/Career Connection

Your decision to come to college is an investment you are making in your future. The true purpose of an education it to set you on a path that will result in how you will lead the rest of your life. We spend most of our lives developing our career. If you graduate from high school at age 17, spend two to four years in college, and then retire at age 67, that means that you will spend 45 – 50 years working (the majority of your life). Since your career takes up such a large percentage of your lifetime, you should think carefully about what you really want to do.

How do you define a career? The Business Dictionary Online (2012) defines a career as "the progression and actions taken by a person throughout a lifetime, especially those related to that person's occupation. A career is often composed of the jobs held, titles earned, and work accomplished over a long period of time …" So in essence, your career is not really defined until it's over and you can look back on what you have accomplished. What do you want to say about your career when you look back? What do you want to be proud of? What do you want to be able to say that you did NOT do? Consider these 'career' quotes (Great Quotes, 2011).

- "Why join the Navy when you can be a pirate?"-Steve Jobs, founder and CEO, Apple Computers

- "Make a career of humanity." -Martin Luther King, Jr., Civil rights activist

- "I should think that being my old lady is all the satisfaction or career any woman needs." -Mick Jagger, rock singer

- "Find out what you do best and then get someone to pay you to do it." -Katherine Whitehorn

- My career should adapt to me." -Leonardo DiCaprio, actor

- I want a big career … I just couldn't stand being anonymous." -Mia Farrow, actress

- "I don't want to get into the habit of thinking about my career … I could die tomorrow." -River Phoenix, actor

Do you identify with any of these quotes when it comes to your career?

Keep in mind that things do not always work out as they were planned, but that should not deter you from making plans. When you were a little kid, you probably dreamed about living a great life surrounded by wonderful people and you wouldn't even have to work. But now it's time to turn those dreams into reality and create a down to earth or realistic plan of action for success.

Your college major is the ladder to your career. If you are undecided in your major you will find yourself in good company. Nationally, 30 to 40 percent of first semester freshmen enter college undecided about what major they should take. In addition, between 70 and 80 percent of students change their major once they are in school. Many do so more than once (University of Missouri – St. Louis, 2011).

Despite the fact that you have not chosen a career, you find yourself in college. Don't feel bad. Your campus career center can assist you in determining what career would be best for you. You may even choose to take a career planning course or workshop.

No matter what major you choose, there is a direct connection between good educational habits and successful career practices. Pursuing a college education is work. In fact, the most successful students have learned to treat their college education as a full-time job. You will come to realize that the higher education process is a precursor for the work environment. The most effective instructors and college institutions will constantly remind you of that fact. This is so important that many colleges and universities include that message in their mission statement.

It is not a coincidence, therefore, that the mission statements of most colleges make reference to how a student's education will enable them to live more productive lives, lead them into a rewarding career, and make a positive contribution to society.

Here is a sample of some of the mission statements of the country's best-known colleges:

- Harvard University: "… to create knowledge, to open the minds of students to that knowledge, and to enable students to take best advantage of their educational opportunities" (Harvard University, 2012).

- Yale University: "…the cultivation of citizens with a rich awareness of our heritage to lead and serve in every sphere of human activity" (Yale University, 2012).

- Atlanta Technical College: "…the integration of academics and applied career preparation to enhance student learning is essential in meeting the workforce demands and economic development needs of the people, businesses, and communities" (Atlanta Technical College, 2012).

- Southern University at Shreveport: "…to provide a quality education for its students, while being committed to the total community" (Southern University at Shreveport 2012).

- Central Piedmont Community College: "…advances the life-long educational development of students consistent with their needs, interests, and abilities while strengthening the economic, social, and cultural life of its diverse community" (Central Piedmont Community College, 2012).

- Amherst College: "…educates men and women of exceptional potential from all backgrounds so that they may seek, value, and advance knowledge, engage the world around them, and lead principled lives of consequence" (Amherst College, 2012).

Student Voices: Tom

Tom is a U.S. Army veteran. He has always wanted to be a chef in his own restaurant. The English composition class he took at his local community college offered the option of participating in a service learning project. As a part of that project, Tom served lunch to 128 men at the Uptown Men's Shelter. He had always thought that he would only be happy serving gourmet meals in a four star restaurant, but when he saw the how appreciative the homeless men were to get a hot meal. Tom started thinking about other places and ways to feed people. His service learning project opened his eyes to people who are less fortunate, but still deserving of the basic necessities of life. Now in his third semester in school, Tom has expanded his volunteer work and spent time at the local food bank and helped out at the homeless shelter to provide meals for all the major holidays. He has even received some catering jobs for his own business by 'rubbing elbows' with some of the other volunteers.

Your Voice:

1. How would the mission statements of the above colleges apply to Tom's experience?

2. What is the mission statement for your college?

3. What can you do to take advantage of what your college has to offer?

UNIT 2
IT'S ABOUT YOU
IN COLLEGE

Unit 2: It's About You in College

What is College?

Do you remember deciding to go to college? What did you think college would be like before you arrived, and where did those expectations come from? For most students, those expectations were formed by a combination of inputs—often very different sorts of inputs: the admiration they felt for an earnest mentor, many serious conversations with parents, and daydreams with friends. These last are often informed by movies - many, many movies: the uproarious anarchy of movies like "Accepted" and "Animal House", or movies like "Van Wilder" and "Back to School," with their transformative arc from hedonism to responsibility, or movies like "Legally Blonde" and "Good Will Hunting," in which improbable characters change from being discounted to being recognized for their genius. Admittedly, it may be difficult for you to find a college that will meet all of those goals, and that may be a good thing.

College holds an iconic place in American culture with good reason. If you are reading this textbook as a part of a college class, you have joined 57% of the American population who have pursued education beyond the high school or GED level (U.S. Census Bureau, 2011). But cultural icons are not merely iconic because they are widespread. They are iconic because they serve important purposes beyond their immediate functions in a society. John Wayne was an iconic actor not because he was in a lot of movies. He was iconic because the characters that John Wayne played embodied myths about "rugged individualism". In many ways, college is a cultural icon that stands for important ideals such as personal growth, transformation and opportunity. It is important to know which ideals you bring to college. This knowledge helps you understand the nature of the outcome you seek. It might also be useful to recognize that these ideals change over time.

Table 2.1
Desired Outcomes of Education 1970 - 2010

Table 2.1

Desired Outcomes of Education 1970-2010

Percent of incoming first year students responding "very important" or "essential"

Characteristic	1970	1980	1990	2000	2010
Personal objectives–very important or essential					
Being very well off financially	36.2	62.5	72.3	73.4	77.4
Developing a meaningful philosophy of life	79.1	62.5	45.9	42.4	46.9
Keeping up to date with political affairs	57.2	45.2	46.6	28.1	33.2

In the table above, we see a dramatic change in what incoming first year students said were their personal objectives for their college experience.

Source: Table 286. Statistical Abstract of the United States. 2012

Table 2.1 shows that in 1970 nearly 4 out of 5 incoming students said it was "very important" or "essential" that they develop a "meaningful philosophy of life" as an outcome of attending college. By 2010, fewer than half of the students stressed that same outcome. Are the students different, or has the social order changed?

Sometimes people use the word "myth" to mean "untruth". Joseph Campbell studied mythology. He used the word myth to describe stories that perform important functions in society. One of those functions is to validate certain types of social order and to align people's stories with that order (Campbell, 1991, p.38).

Myths, Realities and Expectations

It is easy to over-stress the changes represented in Table 2.1. In 2010 nearly half of the students still stressed the need to use their time in college to develop a personal philosophy. And it is important to recognize that these changes in responses are changes in *student expectations*, and do not necessarily reflect changes in student experiences.
The stakes are high. Many students, especially first year students, have unrealistic expectations about college and the way college will help them prepare to take their place in the social order. Some students fit neatly into the roles expected of them. Some do not, and others have no clear idea of what society has to offer, or where they will fit into that society.

Joseph Campbell went on to say,
"...a myth is the society's dream. The myth is the public dream and the dream is the private myth. If ... your dream happens to coincide with that of the society, you are in good accord with your group. If it isn't, you've got an adventure in the dark forest ahead of you" (Campbell, 1991, p. 48).

"An adventure in a dark forest" may sound ominous, or it may sound exciting. It can be either, or both. Your college-educated mentors have found their places in society. They fit. Often, it is that "fit" that we admire so much in mentors. If your parents attended college, they also have found how their own college experience has prepared them for their own places in society, for better or for worse. Of course, your parents' experiences are usually the experiences of a previous generation. Unless your parents attended college in the last ten years, for example, they are probably unfamiliar with on-line registration or email interactions with teachers, and many parents have never heard of some of the new majors, concentrations and courses available today. Students who are first generation college students are also influenced by their parents' expectations of college outcomes, but those expectations are not rooted in college experience."

In all of those cases, however, you will bear responsibility for adjusting your expectations to the realities of the world in which you are finding your way.

Many new students have unrealistic expectations of their own. Only 13.5% of incoming first-year students expect to change majors while in college (UCLA Higher Education Resource Institute, 2009), while more than 50% of students change majors at least once in their college careers (Leonard, 2010).

Colleges look like the population of the age group that enrolls. If you have come to college straight from high school, you will probably find the make-up of college very familiar. Older returning students often find that the demographics of colleges today accurately reflect a new generation in ways they did not expect.

In the long run, adjusting your expectations to the reality of college in the second decade of the 21st Century offers more opportunities than challenges. This is easier if you are open to new experiences because new experiences are really what college offers.

Student Voices: Renee

Like a lot of students, Renee had attended college with a limited view of what would be available to her. She was a first generation college student. Neither of Renee's parents had attended college. In her parents' home country in Southeast Asia, men of her ethnic background were farmers. Even in the United States, men Renee knew rarely attended school. Still, education was seen as an opportunity for women. Two of Renee's aunts and a few female cousins had become nurses. Renee did not really want to become a nurse, but that was the college-career track she grew up hearing about, and the only one her parents knew. When she talked about college with her high school counselor,  nursing was the only career Renee mentioned. Now that she was in college, Renee found that women were talking about all sorts of careers. She had classmates who said they were going to major in accounting, education, pharmacy, or engineering. Renee's parents were very traditional, and so Renee knew her parents would approve of some careers, and not approve of others. She did not want to displease them, and she was worried about exploring other career and major possibilities.

Your Voice:

1. What was the source of Renee's college expectations?

2. What sorts of resources do colleges offer to help students examine their career and major options?

3. What should you do to try to make sure you are open to the possibilities you had not considered before you enrolled in college?

S.M.A.R.T. Goals

If you want to be successful, do what successful people do. One of the things that successful people do is set goals for themselves. A **_goal_** is something that you want to accomplish. We are constantly setting goals for ourselves, either formally or informally.

For many college students, setting a goal is nothing new. You have probably set goals in other areas of your life. See some examples below:

Educational
- Graduate from high school on time.
- Be the first one in my family to attend college.
- Achieve a certain grade point average (GPA) my first semester of college.

Financial:
- Purchase my own car by my 18th birthday.
- Save enough money to travel to Europe this summer.
- Earn enough money to cover tuition and book expenses for a semester.

Career:
- Begin a new career after my children graduate from high school.
- Secure an internship in my career field by the end of the semester.
- Create a resume before I graduate.

Health:
- Run a marathon by the time I am 25.
- Lose 15 pounds before the summer.
- Find and join a gym before I begin my first semester of college.

Now that you are a college student, setting goals takes on new meaning. Goals may be more academic and career focused. College is often viewed as a chance for a "fresh start" in life or a new beginning. For example, if you were a "C" student in high school, maybe college is your chance to become a "B' student. Setting goals is the first step to getting what you want.

Values

The goals that you set are deeply rooted in your own set of personal values, those things that are important to you. These personal values determine how you prioritize your activities and what you decide to devote your time and energy to. So a big part of goal-setting is to examine your own personal values.

What is more important to you in life: achievement or wealth; family life or fame? Values differ from one person to another, and may even change as you gain more life experience. What's important is that you know and understand what you do value in life, and once your values have been established you are prepared to set goals.

The activity on the following page will help you define your values.

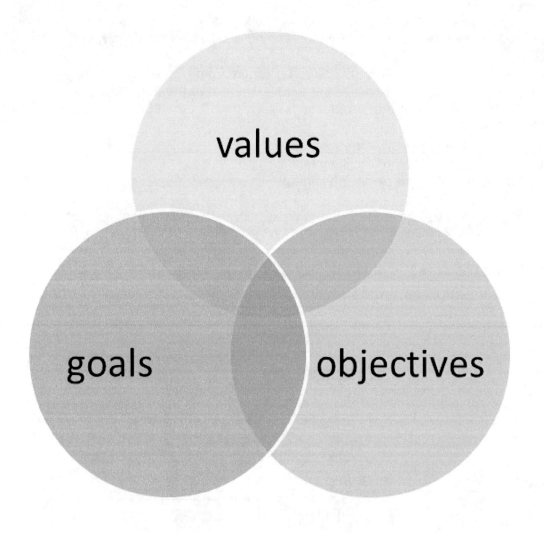

Values Exercise

Directions: Place the following values in the appropriate column for you.

VALUES

Achievement	Advancement	Adventure
Affection	Competitiveness	Cooperation
Creativity	Financial security	Fame
Family life	Freedom	Friendship
Health	Integrity	Loyalty
Order	Physical appearance	Power
Personal development	Pleasure	Self-respect
Spiritual life	Volunteerism	Wealth

LEVEL OF IMPORTANCE

HIGH	MEDIUM	LOW
_____	_____	_____
_____	_____	_____
_____	_____	_____
_____	_____	_____
_____	_____	_____
_____	_____	_____
_____	_____	_____

I discovered that:

_____

_____

_____

_____

S.M.A.R.T.: A system for setting goals

Goal-setting is a very powerful tool that can be used to get you focused and put you on a path to success. An effective way to set meaningful goals is to follow the S.M.A.R.T. process. Goals that you set for yourself should be Specific, Measurable, Attainable, Realistic, and Timely.

When you write out your goals, look them over and make sure that they follow this process. If your goal is lacking in any of these five qualities, just change that goal to include it.

S.M.A.R.T.		
⟶ **S**	Specific	Say exactly what you want.
⟶ **M**	Measurable	How will you know if you did/did not achieve the goal?
⟶ **A**	Attainable	The goal must be within your ability to achieve.
⟶ **R**	Realistic	The goal must be realistic in terms of other aspects and abilities.
⟶ **T**	Timely	The goal must have a reasonable time by which it is realized.

Which of the following goals meets the S.M.A.R.T. criteria?

A.   "I would like to do really well in college."

B.   "I would like to complete all my required courses in English by the end of Spring semester with no less than a "B" in any class."

Goal "B" is specific. The student clearly states what they would like to accomplish.

Goal "B" is measurable. Completing the classes with a grade of B or higher can be measured.

Goal "B" is most likely attainable for the student, and is a realistic goal.

Goal "B" has a timeline of spring semester.

Objectives

Once you have set your goals, you are ready to embark on the second part of the goal setting process: setting objectives. Objectives are specific steps that you plan to take in order to reach your goal. Just like goals, objectives also need to be S. M. A. R. T. Your objectives should be written in such a way as to produce a "to do" list for yourself. This way you can immediately start taking steps to reach your goals.

The goals and objectives worksheet at the end of this chapter is an excellent exercise to use for this process. Specifying objectives will also give you a sense of accomplishment. As you complete your objectives, you get closer to completing your goal. The next thing you know, you have accomplished your goal.

Now it is time for celebration! But don't celebrate too long, because after the completion of one goal, it is time to set another. This is what successful people do. Their lives are a succession of completing one goal after another. Each goal that they set is a little different from or more difficult than the previous one. As they continue to accomplish one goal after another, they realize that their options expand and that they can do new things. The same can be true for you.

Barriers to Goal-Setting

Goal-setting seems like such an easy process, so why isn't everybody doing it? Most people are not because there are barriers that get in the way of achieving goals. These barriers can be created by situations, friends and relatives, and sometimes even ourselves. If you plan ahead, you can accurately predict some of the obstacles that might stand in your way and take steps to prevent them.

Setting your Goals and Objectives

List one goal you would like to pursue in the next five years. Your goal should meet the S.M.A.R. T. criteria (*Specific – Measurable –Attainable – Realistic – Timely*). Avoid the use of general words such as "more," "better," or "less."

Example: I want to complete English 111 by the end of next semester with a grade of A or B.

1. _____

Objectives:
Now write five objectives. Objectives are specific steps to take in order to reach your goal.

Example: I will turn in any required English assignments on or before the due date.

1. _____

2. _____

3. _____

4. _____

5. _____

Things to do:
Generate a "to do" list of things that you can do right away to reach your objectives.

Example: I will use a planner to list all due dates for English assignments this semester.

1. _____

2. _____

3. _____

4. _____

5. _____

Overcoming Barriers to Success

One way to overcome barriers to success is to identify them and take steps to overcome them. Using the goal that you have previously stated, identify at least one potential barrier that might stand in your way as you endeavor to pursue that goal. Then list one strategy for overcoming each of these barriers. Use complete sentences.

Goal: _____

Potential barriers:
Example: My job hours change every week which keeps me from getting classes during the day/night.

1. _____

2. _____

3. _____

4. _____

5. _____

Strategies to overcome barriers:
Example: Lock into a permanent schedule with my boss for the semester or get a different job.

1. _____

2. _____

3. _____

4. _____

5. _____

Student voices: Kyle

Kyle had always dreamed of playing professional sports. Unfortunately, an injury during a high school football game crushed his hopes of doing that. As a college student, Kyle realized that he still wanted to remain involved in the sports field, and decided that he could become a sportscaster for ESPN, or even for a local news channel. He had seen many professional athletes who had become commentators and believed that he could pursue that goal, as well.

One of Kyle's instructors at the college suggested that he meet with a career counselor to help him choose the best major for his career. Kyle was surprised to learn that one of his degree options was journalism, and that it involved courses is English, writing and public speaking. What Kyle was discovering, was that athletic experience and knowledge of sports played just a small part in his career requirements, and that academics played a major role.

For Kyle, the goal setting process was just beginning. His new long-term SMART goal was to complete a degree in journalism within five years. Once his goal was set, he could move forward with creating a list of steps or "objectives" which would bring him closer to his goal. Selecting and registering for classes seemed like the logical next step for Kyle. What would he need to know in order to do that?

What Kyle discovered was that his dream had the potential of becoming a reality. It was an exciting discovery, but it was going to take work. Kyle was starting to see that setting and accomplishing goals was a step by step process. He recalled the words of one of his favorite athletes, Michael Jordan: ..."If [your goal is to become a doctor]...and you're getting C's in biology then the first thing you have to do is get B's in biology and then A's. You have to perfect the first step and then move on to chemistry or physics."

(Jordan and Vancil, 1994)

He was motivated to go back and look up the quote in context.

"I approach everything step by step....I had always set short-term goals. As I look back, each one of the steps or successes led to the next one. When I got cut from the varsity team as a sophomore in high school, I learned something. I knew I never wanted to feel that bad again....So I set a goal of becoming a starter on the varsity. That's what I focused on all summer. When I worked on my game, that's what I thought about. When it happened, I set another goal, a reasonable, manageable goal that I could realistically achieve if I worked hard enough....I guess I approached it with the end in mind. I knew exactly where I wanted to go, and I focused on getting there. As I reached those goals, they built on one another. I gained a little confidence every time I came through.

...If [your goal is to become a doctor]...and you're getting Cs in biology then the first thing you have to do is get B's in biology and then As. You have to perfect the first step and then move on to chemistry or physics.

Take those small steps. Otherwise you're opening yourself up to all kinds of frustration. Where would your confidence come from if the only measure of success was becoming a doctor? If you tried as hard as you could and didn't become a doctor, would that mean your whole life was a failure? Of course not. All those steps are like pieces of a puzzle. They all come together to form a picture....Not everyone is going to be the greatest....But you can still be considered a success....Step by step, I can't see any other way of accomplishing anything."

(Jordan and Vancil, 1994)

Your voice:

1. How can Kyle use the SMART process of goal setting to make sure he completes his degree within five years?

2. Kyle dreamed of playing professional sports. What is the difference between having a dream and having a goal?

3. Which of your dreams can become an achievable goal for you?

Study Skills

In college, you are in control of how your time is spent. Along with college comes the freedom to make choices. Choices about your classes, choices about attendance, choices about studying and choices about completing your course work for each class.

Consider some of the choices students make during the semester.

- How often will I attend class?
- On which days will I study?
- Will I spend my weekends working, studying or socializing?
- Will I focus only on course work , or will I also do the required reading for each course?
- How long will I study?
- How will I remember due dates and test dates?

The choices you make will affect your level of success in each class you take. Good choices often lead to success, whereas poor choices tend to result in consequences.

One of the biggest challenges for college students is learning how to manage their time more efficiently. Since many college students are taking a full course load, working a full or part time job, or perhaps raising a family, time management is a major concern. Consider this: "Carrying a full load of college credits is essentially equivalent to having a full-time job! " (Duke 2012)

In order to fully understand and master the course content according to your instructor's expectations, you should expect to study between two and three hours for every hour you spend in class. You are in control of how each of the 24 hours in a day is spent. If you are taking a full course load in college, or 12-15 credit hours, then the time you spend studying should equal 24-30 hours per week.

This might include:

- Required course reading
- Daily homework
- Projects
- Preparing for quizzes and exams
- Writing assignments
- Tutoring
- Study group time
- Class organization

How do college students manage to fit those activities, and more, into 24 hours? Effective time management comes from establishing your priorities and planning your activities.

According to Stephen Covey, author of *The Seven Habits of Highly Successful People*, prioritizing is all about putting "first things first." What are first things? "First things are those things you, personally, find most worth." (Covey, 1989)

Prioritizing your activities allow you to:

- be in control of your time
- decide what is most important to you
- choose the plan
- change the plan
- accomplish our most important tasks
- accomplish small daily goals
- procrastinate less
- stop worrying about when things will get done
- decrease the stress that comes from running out of time
- build self-discipline
- build self-confidence
- maintain a sense of accomplishment

Establishing Your Priorities:

The first step is the most important. Your priorities are personal to you. You decide which activities are the most important to you and you always find a way to get those things done. A good way to prioritize your activities is to first list all of the activities that you do on a regular basis. Then categorize them into three groups: *must do, should do,* and *could do. Must do* activities are things that are vital and have utmost importance. *Should do* activities are important but are not critical. *Could do* activities are things that you would like to do but not immediately. The activities that go into these categories come from personal preference.

Step 1: Establish your priorities

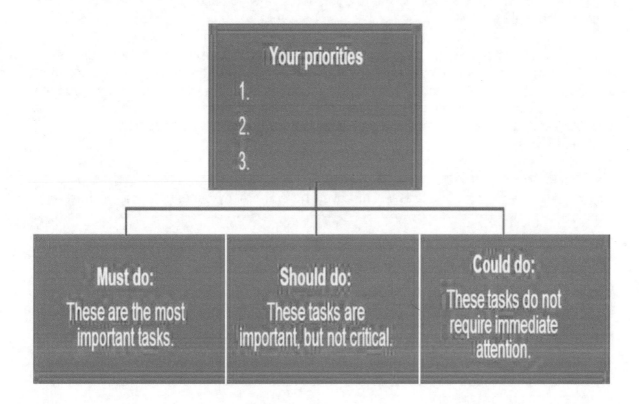

Step 2: Plan your activities

Once you have prioritized your activities, it is time to schedule them. Use a planner, weekly calendar or electronic device to schedule your activities. First, schedule time for the activities you *must do*. These required commitments often include class time, work schedules, study times and sleeping. Next, schedule regular times for the activities you *should do* to ensure that they get done. These activities may include appointments, errands, or personal commitments that can be worked around your class or job schedule. Finally, allow some time for the activities you *could do*. Remember, they do not require immediate attention, but they need to be completed.

You can formalize this schedule by entering it in a planner, or by keeping up with it informally. Either way, you should take some time to think about how you spend your time. Taking time to save time makes sense.

Learning how to effectively manage your time is a process, not an event. You will need to repeat this process over and over again, and make changes when necessary. As you continue to practice planning and prioritizing, your time management skills will improve. Soon you may find that you have enough time to get everything done and even have some extra time to do some of the things that you have always wanted to do. It all starts with establishing your priorities.

The benefits of prioritizing and planning

As you take time to save time, you will discover there are many benefits. Some of these include:

Free time - Prioritizing and planning your activities during specific times of the day may result in gaining some "free time" or "down time".

Motivation - Establishing a plan can be motivating. If you are a procrastinator, a plan can help you get started with your activities.

Better study habits - Setting specific times for studying and reviewing course material can motivate you to do daily and weekly reviews, instead of just cramming the day before the exam.

Stress reduction - Stress and anxiety can be reduced by having a plan in place. Once your priorities have been established for the day, there is no need to worry about what has to be done. If you are worried about being tied down by your daily plan, consider this: You are in charge of your plan. You have prioritized each task and have set up a plan of action. At any time, you can reevaluate and revise your plan. Be sure to build in some fun time, as well. All students need time to relax and recharge.

Assess your planning skills.

In each of the following pairs, choose the statement that sounds most like you:

A. I make a daily to-do list.
B. I go through each day without a plan.

A. I use a calendar, planner or electronic calendar.
B. I keep date, appointments and assignments "in my head".

A. I write exam dates, test dates and due dates in a planner.
B. I rely on the professor to remind me of these dates.

A. I write appointments and errands in a planner or calendar.
B. I remember them without writing them down.

A. I schedule times for homework, studying or course reading.
B. I complete homework and study when I feel like it.

A. I allow time for relaxation and fun.
B. I put fun and relaxation first, and fit in course work when I can.

If you chose mostly "A"s, you may already be planning effectively. If you chose mostly "B"s, you may be accomplishing your tasks, but needlessly adding stress and uncertainty.

Prioritizing My Activities

Directions: Rank the following activities from 1 to 10 in order of priority to you. Be prepared to discuss why you ranked the activity as you did.

_____ You have a chemistry exam tomorrow morning that you've known about for a week.

_____ Your two-page English paper is due tomorrow afternoon.

_____ A friend calls and needs your help with algebra right away!

_____ There is a Spanish test tomorrow morning that the teacher announced in class today.

_____ You are the president of the drama club, and the meeting is tonight at 8:00.

_____ You promised your girlfriend/boyfriend that you would finally spend some time with her/him tonight.

_____ You don't have any clean socks. You need to do laundry.

_____ You have a history paper due in two days, but there is concert out of town that you were planning to attend.

_____ You usually visit your mother once a week, and you missed last week.

_____ You really need some sleep.

Prioritize the above activities in the chart below.

Must Do	Should do	Could do

Successful Students

Once students register for classes, a different type of "work" begins. Just like a job or a career, taking classes in college demands certain traits of students.

What do you think some of the characteristics of a successful student might be?

10 Characteristics of Successful Students

1. _____

2. _____

3. _____

4. _____

5. _____

6. _____

7. _____

8. _____

9. _____

10. _____

What are some of the characteristics of unsuccessful students?

10 Characteristics of Unsuccessful Students

1. _____

2. _____

3. _____

4. _____

5. _____

6. _____

7. _____

8. _____

9. _____

10. _____

Success Strategies in College

There are so many books written about how to be a successful student, you would think it was a complicated endeavor. It is not really that complicated. The truth is that there are ten things you can do to greatly enhance your ability to be successful in the courses you take. Whether you are taking a traditional (seated) or online class, these strategies apply.

1. **Show up.**

   The very first day of class, *be there*. No matter *who* tells you that it does not matter if you attend the first day or week, that advice is **wrong**. Your attendance tells your instructor right from the beginning that you are serious about being in college. Granted, there are circumstances such as late registration (if it exists at your school) that may prohibit your attendance the first day, but arriving in class long after class has begun sends a clear message that this class is just not that important to you. If you do not think first impressions are important, think about how you would feel if your instructor did not show up the first week. Even if attendance is not part of your grade, you will miss vital information when you miss *any* class.

   For online classes, showing up means logging into the course on the first day or during that first week. Regularly accessing the course online is necessary in most online courses to be considered "in attendance."

   Most colleges have a date by which students MUST be present in class in order to be enrolled. Some state reporting procedures require students to be in class by a certain date or they are reported to the state as "Never Attending." Students who do not show up by the required date may lose their enrollment in the class which may affect their financial aid status. Check the dates and deadlines for attendance at your college to make sure that you are not making a critical assumption.

   "Eighty percent of success is showing up." Woody Allen, screenwriter, director, actor

2. **Be prepared.**

   Be prepared to give your full, uninterrupted attention to the dynamics of the class so that you can extract the important information you need for discussions and future exams. Make sure you get enough sleep before class so that you are awake and alert. Being prepared also means that you complete the assigned reading, bring the materials you need to follow along from the textbook, participate in lab activities, take notes, and change due dates in your planner. If you are hungry, grab a snack and eat it *before* class begins. Use the restroom and make all phone calls and text messages before or after your time with the instructor in class. You have paid for this educational moment, which can never be reproduced. Take advantage of the full scope of the class.

   Being prepared for online classes means that you are certain you have access to a computer and the internet for the entire term. It also includes purchasing the required book and materials the instructor has specified. Prepare for your time in the online course; make sure outside distractions are eliminated while you work online.

The syllabus is the most important document and your reference for assignments and course requirements in traditional and online classes. Make sure you always have a copy of the syllabus.

"The secret of success is to be ready when your opportunity comes."
Benjamin Disraeli, (1804-1881), British Prime Minister

3. Take notes.

Even if you are an auditory learner, you can benefit from the kinesthetic and visual experience of taking notes in class. If you are the student who never takes notes in class, you may have noticed that most of the information you heard was forgotten in 24 hours. Sure, you will remember the highlights, but it is the details and connections to other concepts that make the difference in essay exams and class discussions. There are lots of different ways to take notes – many of which can suit your learning style.

Find the ones you like and use them every time you attend a class. Remember to experiment with different note-taking methods to keep your attention level high.

For online classes, taking notes takes on a whole new meaning. Note-taking may include setting up a bookmark folder. You may take traditional notes to accompany a taped lecture or a link to a video clip. It may mean that you want to copy and paste some material into a Microsoft Word document later for studying. It may mean highlighting parts of the course. Whichever way you notate important material, make sure that you are organizing and filing so you know where to find it later.

"He listens well who takes notes."
Dante Alighieri, poet, writer, philosopher, (Brainy Quote, 2012)

4. Plan ahead.

Figure out what you want to do, and which classes you want and need. There are advisors and counselors who can help you do *all* of that. You can always ask your classmates and friends who are in school with you, but keep in mind that their learning styles may be different from yours. With proper planning, you can avoid classes you are not prepared to take. It costs time and money to take classes by mistake. This is especially true for students who think they are ready for an online class. Do not wait until the last minute to sign up for classes. It is important to know that many classes fill up early. If your employer, financial aid, or insurance requires you to be a full-time student, the best way to make certain you have the hours you need is to *plan ahead*. Registration begins long before the semester begins. Successful students register early in the registration period. It is never too early to plan ahead.

For online classes, planning ahead means making sure that you have planned your online time well. Eliminate distractions, secure your internet connection, and set aside enough time to take timed tests. There is a difference between self-paced and online classes. Online classes may have due dates and expirations times for materials to be available. Self-paced classes often grant the student full access to the entire course from beginning to end of term and may allow for the student to complete the work required *at their own pace*. **Do not assume that your course is self-paced**.

"The beginning is the most important part of the work."
Plato (BC 427-BC 347) Greek philosopher

5. **Check a limiting attitude at the door.**

Students come to college for many reasons. Some are here because they want or need an education. Some students come because they are told they must. Others come because they want to impress someone or to be a part of a culture to which they think they belong. Regardless of the reason, students bring their attitudes about education with them. Some of these attitudes may unnecessarily limit your opportunity for success. Those opportunities begin the minute you allow yourself to be open-minded about the instructor, the classroom environment, classmates, or notions about what college *should* be like.

For online classes, the same cautions apply. Sometimes, students assume an online class will be easy. That assumption may lead to resentment when they discover that many aspects of on-line classes require more work and self-discipline than traditional classes. Often, students who register for online classes do so to avoid interaction with other students. Students often have more direct interaction with other students if the instructor is using discussion boards and group projects online.

"Begin challenging your own assumptions. Your assumptions are your windows on the world. Scrub them off every once in a while, or the light won't come in." Alan Alda, actor

6. **Become involved.**

Students who sit in the front of the class are more likely to be involved in lecture, classroom discussions and activities. It is difficult to fall asleep or fade into oblivion when you are front and center. Being able to contribute to discussions helps you stabilize information in auditory, visual, and kinesthetic learning styles. Being involved means more than contributing in class. It also implies that your success depends on involvement within the college community through academics and extra-curricular activities. Students who make friends in their classes or on their campus draw support from those relationships and establish potential long-term connections.

For online classes, involvement requires participation in discussion boards and communication with other students. Treat those communications as if you were in a seated class. Use e-mail etiquette and remember that there are *people* at the receiving end of your messages.

"If you're not actively involved in getting what you want, you don't really want it." Peter McWilliams, author

7. Get to know your instructor.

It is strange to think that the person who is instructing your class was once sitting in a first year class, just like the one you are in now. Imagine what he or she may have been like in the first few semesters of college. Students often forget that to get where they are now, instructors had to overcome many of the same obstacles that students do today. One of the best ways to become successful in any course is to get to know your instructor. After a particularly interesting session during the beginning of a semester, spend a few moments to tell your instructor what you liked about the class that day. It may spark a conversation that will open a line of communication between you and the instructor that can come in handy if you have a particularly difficult time with the material later. In the same manner that you learn to "check a limiting attitude at the door," try postponing judgment about the instructor until you have spent more time in the class.

For online classes, getting to know your instructor is a function of your e-mail and assignment submissions. If your instructor provides an office phone number, you might want to call them to discuss an assignment or to offer a good word about what you like about the course. Stop by their office, if it is convenient, so that you can introduce yourself. Putting a face or a voice with a name is a great way to help your instructor remember you.

"You want to remember that while you're judging the book, the book is also judging you." Stephen King, author

8. Do not procrastinate.

Listen to conversations with your classroom peers and inevitably you will hear them talk about the stress and chaos of procrastination. Often they will say things like, "I work better under pressure" or "If I wait until the last minute, I do a better job of focusing on the work." The truth is, procrastination is the killer of *great* things. Granted, you can do some *good* things and get them done just in time, but you will never know how truly great they *could* have been had you proofread and edited them (even asked another person to look over your work) before submission. Instructors can usually distinguish the work that is done with care and precision from work thrown together at the last minute. That is why some students get A's and B's and some get C's, D's, and F's. Have you ever known someone who has studied diligently throughout the semester and has confidence to take an exam? Do you know someone who stayed up all night and tried to cram everything from the entire semester into his or her short term memory to try to get a "decent" grade on the final? Whose grade would you rather have?

For online classes, the suggestion to not procrastinate is vital. Students who assume that they can make up the work anytime within the term will discover that often, that is not the case. Again, unless the class is defined as a self-paced class, expect to find due dates for assignments and projects.

"Procrastination makes easy things hard, hard things harder."
Mason Cooley, American aphorist, professor emeritus, College of Staten Island, Columbia University

9. Do not ask if you missed anything after missing a week's worth of classes.

Even if you just missed a day, you missed something. It was important. It may or may not be on the test, but it was still important. You are responsible for work you miss. Check with your classmates, check with your instructor, and check Blackboard, Moodle, or whichever learning management system is used by your school. Always check to make sure you are getting accurate information. Do not assume that you will be able to turn in late work. Refer to your class syllabus for policies regarding submission of late work.

For online classes, the suggestions are the same as for traditional classes. Make no assumptions and do not procrastinate.

"You can tell whether a man is clever by his answers. You can tell whether a man is wise by his questions." Naguib, Mahfouz, Egyptian writer, Nobel Prize winner

10. Speaking of, "Will it be on the test?"

In most classes *everything* is fodder for the test. If you have followed the previous nine suggestions, however, and practice student success strategies, you should be able to recognize most of the likely exam topics. More importantly, you will learn that taking exams is not the true measure of learning. You will learn much more in life than you will ever find on a test.

For online classes, students often make the assumption that the test content comes from the written work submitted. Remember that discussion boards, wikis, blogs and other assignments are included in that written work. Instructors know you do not have time to waste, and neither do they. The work you do in a discussion board has a purpose and an outcome. Using the information that you learned through a discussion board on a test is a great way to let the instructor know that you were engaged in the learning that took place in the online class.

"The man who graduates today and stops learning tomorrow is uneducated the day after." Newton D. Baker (1871-1937), American politician, Secretary of War

Your Academic Plan

Now that you have gathered some information about who you are and what you would like to do, it is time to put together a plan of action. You have come to college to accomplish a goal- to become a successful student and create a lucrative and satisfying career. Most people do not plan to fail, they fail to plan. Your next step is to put together an academic plan to help ensure your success as a college student.

Today, both jobs and careers usually depend on a certificate, a degree or a diploma. In 2009, the U.S. Department of Labor (2012) reported that 62% of all U.S. jobs now require a two or four year degree and higher, *or* post-secondary occupational certificates or apprenticeships. By 2020, we can expect that percentage to increase to 75%. Today's students are participating in a global economy. That means that they work and compete with people and technology from all over the world.

College is where students acquire skills and professional socialization to ready themselves for their careers. It is not enough to simply know *how* to do something. We must also be able to relate to other human beings and understand them.

Student Voices: Carlos

Carlos' family has been involved in the medical profession for many years. Carlos knows that becoming a nurse will require an education past high school and several years in some tough math and science classes. He has seen some of his family members choose jobs and careers that do not require post-secondary education and still have great lives. Carlos has remained dedicated to a college education and his career goal. He works on a part-time basis doing small errands and light clerical work at the clinic where his mother is employed. This experience reinforces his decision to work in the medical field, and he enjoys wearing scrubs, working alongside the professionals in the clinic.

Carlos' level of self-confidence is high because of his experience at the clinic, but he is unaware that his people skills are a problem for the staff. Carlos' self-confidence overwhelms the reality of his abilities. He wants to take on more responsibilities, but without the degree or certification required by the state, his job is somewhat limited. Both he and the staff at the clinic know that he may be *capable* of many of the tasks at the clinic, but state regulations will prohibit Carlos from doing them.

During a staffing shortage, Carlos offered to help out in the clinical examining room. He was politely, but adamantly turned down because he was uncertified. As one physician put it, "Carlos, you have great promise in this field and certainly you have the ability, but without the license to perform these tasks, we simply cannot let you help."

Carlos' frustration became evident in his verbal communication with other staff members and his body language about the tasks he was given to complete. Sweeping and taking out the trash just did not make him feel like he was part of the solution to healthcare issues.

After enrolling in a few classes at the community college, Carlos began to meet other students with similar medical career goals. Listening to his classmates as they discussed their goals, Carlos realized that his experience working in the medical clinic was unique and valuable.   He could use this practical experience to leverage his candidacy for the nursing program at the college.

What was once merely a dream for him has become a potential reality--if he has the courage to take the necessary steps to complete the required coursework successfully. He needs a plan.

Your Voice:

1. Why does Carlos think he can perform tasks that are relegated only to individuals that have a degree or certification in the medical field?

2. What assumptions do students make about the requirements needed to be eligible for certain careers? What faulty reasoning is used to reinforce these incorrect assumptions?

3. How do skills and professional socialization help direct your career path?

Compiling your Educational Genealogy and writing a personal narrative should have helped prepare you for writing your academic plan. Your plan is your guide. It should lead you to the goals you identify, and help you achieve what you desire from college.

For the next step, you will need to focus on those desires.

1. What was your dream job when you were little?

2. What are your likes and dislikes?

3. Which career field interests you?

4. What is your current major?

5. What are the skills required to be successful in this field?

6. What will you do when you are finished with your courses at this college?

7. At which companies or institutions would you like to work?

The answers to the next questions will help identify your next steps. You will also need to reexamine your intentions and your realities to see if this is indeed, the right career path for you. Many people go to college and major in something that appears interesting or pays a lot of money, but they are not sure if this is the field in which they want to work. This is something that you will need to think about before going too far in your coursework, otherwise, you may end up wasting time and money.

1. How do you plan to complete your academic goal?

2. How many semesters will it take you to complete your studies?

3. When will you be ready to transfer to another school, if this is your goal?

4. How many hours of classes can you realistically take each semester and still keep your life in balance?

These answers will help you to devise a realistic plan to determine which classes you should take each semester and then predict a completion date.

Pursuing a college education is a big task. Big tasks seem achievable once a plan of action is devised and set in motion. This is your plan of action. It may not play out exactly as you have devised it and changes will need to be made along the way, but you have to start somewhere.

An academic plan is a great place to start.

What is Your Major?

Most students claim a major without first giving it careful thought. This topic is too important to be left to impulse. You should take time to consider the implications of your major choice. Majors lead to careers. You can use the grid on the following page to gather information and contemplate your career choice. It is important to answer the questions honestly. You may want to ask someone who knows you well to help you answer.

Here are the questions. Use this list to gather information before putting filling out the grid.

1. What is your current major?

2. What are 5 attributes (qualities, characteristics or features) or skills (abilities) that someone in this major must have to be successful?

3. Who are 5 people who currently work in this field?

4. What are 5 prominent companies/industries/services in this field? Where are they located?

5. What are your 5 best qualities or skills?

6. What are 5 skills that you need to improve?

7. How do you plan to improve these skills?

8. What are your top 5 barriers to success?

9. How will you eliminate or diminish these barriers?

10. Who can help you work on these skills and barriers?

Choosing Your Major

Complete the grid with information about your current career choice. The information that you provide in the chart will help you take a realistic look at the preparation you have done or need to do to move toward that goal.

Major	5 Best Attributes	5 People in field	5 Companies /locations	5 best skills	5 Skills I need to improve	Ways to improve each skill	Who can help me?

Planning Your Courses

Next Term Academic Plan

Name:

_____

Date:

_____

- The program I plan to complete is_____.

- Are the classes in this program designed to transfer to another college or university?
  ☐ Yes   ☐ No

  If yes, I plan to transfer to _____ and major in _____.

☐ I should contact my Advisor to help me select courses each term.

Name:_____

Office:_____

Phone number:_____

☐ *I need to submit an official high school transcript to the Student Records office and request transcript evaluation to be enrolled in my program and meet all requirements.*

	Classes *I am taking this term*	Classes *I need to take*
English		
Math		
Science		
Electives		
Other		

Expanded Academic Plan

Now that you have completed your course schedule for next term, you should create an expanded academic plan through completion.

How many credit hours of courses can you <u>realistically</u> handle each term? _____

Based on these hours, write a plan to complete your field of study.

Term _____

Class	Hours
_____	_____
_____	_____
_____	_____
_____	_____
_____	_____

Term _____

Class	Hours
_____	_____
_____	_____
_____	_____
_____	_____
_____	_____

Term _____

Class	Hours
_____	_____
_____	_____
_____	_____
_____	_____
_____	_____

Term _____

Class	Hours
_____	_____
_____	_____
_____	_____
_____	_____
_____	_____

Term _____

Term _____

Class	Hours	Class	Hours
_____	_____	_____	_____
_____	_____	_____	_____
_____	_____	_____	_____
_____	_____	_____	_____
_____	_____	_____	_____

Term _____	Term _____

Class	Hours	Class	Hours
_____	_____	_____	_____
_____	_____	_____	_____
_____	_____	_____	_____
_____	_____	_____	_____
_____	_____	_____	_____

Projected Completion Date

When do you plan to complete your degree or transfer? _____

NOTES:

_____

_____

_____

_____

_____

_____

College/Career Connection
General Education Goals

To be successful in college, students need to set academic goals and create objectives to help them to reach their goals. This is also true for colleges. Every college has learning goals and objectives for its students. Here are the general education goals of a few colleges and universities:

"... a sound intellectual foundation in the liberal arts and sciences and in the student's chosen major field of study."   (University of Missouri-Columbia, 2012)

"...to connect a student's liberal education -- that is, an education conducted in a spirit of free inquiry, rewarding in its own right -- to life beyond college ..."   (Harvard College, 2012)

" ... help students grow into mature, thoughtful, and engaged members of both the campus community and society as a whole ..."   (Amherst College, 2012)

" ... to give students a solid command of basic principles, a versatility of insight and perspective concerning natural and social phenomena, the habit of continued learning, and the power that comes from a thorough and systematic approach to learning ..."
                              (Massachusetts Institute of Technology, 2012)

" ... provides multiple, varied, and intentional learning experiences to facilitate the acquisition of fundamental knowledge and skills and the development of attitudes that foster effective citizenship and life-long learning."   (Miami Dade Community College, 2012)

What are the general education goals of your college?

Colleges aim to meet their general education goals through a variety of learning objectives and outcomes. Some of these objectives include:

- preparing students for civic engagement

- encouraging critical and creative thinking

- inspiring students to value ethical dimensions

- applying and integrating methods of analysis to real world problems

- helping students to understand themselves in an ever-changing world

How do the faculty, staff, and administrators bring about these changes in students? They first help students assess their skills and then they help students enhance or gain additional skills they will need to meet their goals. There are several skills assessments embedded in the basic processes of all colleges.

Skills Assessments and Transferrable Skills

First, students need a certain level of skills just to gain admission to a college. The assessment tools vary from SAT and ACT scores, to placement tests and basic skills assessments. If you think back to your initial college intake process, you are sure to remember going over at least one of these hurdles. Once students have their initial assessment, they are ready to be placed into courses and begin their journey into higher education.

Now the next level of skills assessment can begin. Students need an initial level of skills just to enroll in certain courses, and they are expected to gain additional skills in the course. Each course has specific learning outcomes that students are required to meet in order to pass. Look at your course syllabus for any one of the courses you are taking this semester. What are the learning outcomes for your current courses?

A third level of skills assessment is taking place while you are on your higher education journey. With each course, you are learning, improving, and refining your overall skill set. You are learning the skills you will need to obtain employment in your selected career. You are improving your existing skills through practice (homework and assignments). You are refining the skills necessary to survive and thrive in society through social interaction and problem solving. Acquiring and transforming your set of skills is really what education is all about. These are lifelong or transferrable skills that you will be able to take into your career. Long after the assignments, tests, deadlines, and graduation are over, this set of transferrable skills will stay with you.

Each course you take will give you content and practice as you develop your skills. Your ability to master these skills will help you pass each course. Transferrable skills will help you to stay in college and complete your course of study.

There are basically six categories of transferrable skills:

1. working with other people

2. effective communication (oral and written)

3. dealing with data (analytical skills)

4. dealing with things (motor skills)

5. leadership

6. taking care of oneself

Use the following checklist to help you identify your transferrable skills.

Transferrable Skills Checklist (Rogue Community College, 2012)

Key Transferrable Skills	Dealing with Things	Working with People	Leadership	Dealing with data	Taking Care of Oneself
- Meet deadlines - Delegating - Planning - Results oriented - Customer service - Supervision - Increasing sales - Accept responsibility - Instruct others - Desire to learn - Desire to improve - Time management - Problem solving - Managing money - Managing budgets - Meeting the public - Organizing people - Managing people - Team player - Writing - Independent worker - Computer skills	- Use your hands - Assembly - Safety - Construct - Repair - Build or observe - Inspection - Feeding machinery - Following Instructions - Operating tools - Operating machinery - Driving vehicles - Operating vehicles - Repairing things - Using complex equipment	- Patient - Caring - Persuasive - Confronting others - Pleasant - Counseling others - Sensitive - Demonstrating - Supportive - Diplomatic - Outgoing - Speaking in public - Negotiating - Helping others - Tactful - Insightful - Teaching - Interviewing - Anticipating needs - High energy - Open Minded - Kind - Taking orders - Listening - Serving - Trusting - Understanding - Adaptable	- Arranging social functions - Motivating people - Negotiating - Decisive - Planning - Delegating - Running meetings - Directing others - Explaining to others - Self-motivated - Getting results - Sharing leadership - Thinking of others - Directing projects - Team building - Solving problems - Mediating problems	- Analyze data - Analyze facts - Investigation - Auditing records - Keeping financial records - Getting answers - Balancing accounts - Managing money - Finding information - Classify data - Comparing facts - Inspect facts - Recording facts - Counting - Observing - Researching - Detail-oriented - Taking inventory	- Articulate - Innovative - Logical - Remembers - Accurate - Dancing - Body movement - Performing - Drawing - Sketching - Artistic - Plays instrument - Expressive

Student Voices: Tom

When Tom decided to go to college his goals were clear:

- to obtain an Associate's Degree in Culinary Arts in two years

- to improve and sharpen his culinary skills

- to obtain employment in a corporate restaurant or hotel company upon graduation

Now that he has been in college for a little over a year, he realizes that his goals left much to be desired. There are numerous other items that should have been included on his goals list.

When it comes to culinary skills, Tom is very confident in his abilities. His coursework has taught him that there are other skills he will need to acquire and improve in order to become a corporate chef. For example, from Tom's experience, a chef needs to 'strike fear in the hearts of all kitchen employees to be a successful manager. He is now learning cooperative and collaborative methods of leadership and supervision. Tom has no problem when it comes to writing menus, recipes, or prep lists, but the Professional Research and Reporting class he will be required to take next semester actually scares him. He has quickly realized he is seriously lacking in some of the vital skills he will need to become a corporate chef. At first, this realization worried him. Was this the right career path for him? Had he taken on too big of a task? Searching for answers, Tom scheduled a meeting with his faculty advisor to discuss his concerns. He felt so much better when his advisor told him she felt the same way years ago when she decided to go back to school.

Instead of feeling inadequate because of his lack of some vital skills, Tom has made a commitment to identify, assess, and improve upon those skills. He still feels confident with his culinary skills, and is now motivated to improve in other areas. His faculty advisor told him, "That is what education is all about."

Your voice:

1. What did Tom do to change his attitude about his lack of skills?

2. What are some of the 'transferrable skills' that Tom lacked?

3. How can you improve your transferrable skills through your coursework?

Career Options

Once you have assessed your skills, you will naturally begin to think about whether your skill set is suitable for your chosen career. If you have not yet determined a career path, your skill set can serve as an indication of which career might suit you. Attention to detail, analytical aptitude and the ability to work with others may be an indication that engineering, business management, or teaching might be good fields for you. The ability to delegate, self-motivation, and fact-seeking are skills that would serve legal professionals, information technology specialists, and accountants well. Look at some of the job descriptions for careers you are considering. Education, experience, and skills are usually listed under the requirements section of the job description. Assessing your current skill level, identifying the skill set required for certain jobs, and working to attain, improve, and enhance your skills will make you a viable candidate for employment.

Student Voices: LaTonya

When LaTonya was in the 10th grade she went on a field trip to the National Air and Science Museum in Washington, DC. She really did not want to go on the field trips. She had no interest in science, although she had an A in her science class. She went because she could get a full day out of her other classes. LaTonya quickly got bored with all the exhibits, wandered away from the group, and ended up in another part of the museum where she could overhear a few of the employees talking. They were all talking about how hard it was to get hired at the museum. If it were not for their college degrees they would not have been hired. LaTonya was shocked to hear that most of the museum employees held college degrees – even the security guards. That is when it happened – LaTonya decided right then that she would also attend college.

Now that LaTonya is a freshman in college, she realizes that just getting into college is not enough. She really needs to pick a major so that she can effectively select her classes, but she has no idea about what she wants to do. When she did go to Career Services they asked her what she wanted to do, and she honestly answered them with, "I have no idea".

Your voice

1. Why is LaTonya having such a hard time determining what her major should be?

2. Which resources are available at your school to help you determine your major?

3. How do you know that you are choosing (have chosen) the right major?

Declaring Your Major

Many students enter college with an undeclared major. You may be one of them. Admissions officers and first year experience instructors know this is not a big problem, but students will soon need to declare their major so they can start taking courses to complete their degree. This should be done at least by the end of the student's sophomore year. Many students really have no idea what they want to major in, mostly because they have no idea about what type of career they want after graduation. Students can go to the Career Center to research careers and take assessments to see which career might best suit them. Still, other students decide to major in general studies or liberal arts because they cannot decide.

A little research will help you to choose a major that will be interesting to you, lead you to a promising career, and set you on the path to complete your college career. Sometimes when students declare a major, they realize that it is not offered at the college they are currently attending. This means they might have to transfer to another college.

The designation "2-year" or "4-year" college implies that it takes students two or four years to complete their degree. In reality, it usually takes longer than that due to dropped/failed classes, remedial or developmental prerequisites, or other problems that cause students to decrease their course load for each semester. Students sometimes find that they must adjust their course load each semester to graduate on time.

Unit 3:
It's About
Your College

It's About Your College

Just as your education began with goals and ideals, colleges and universities have proud traditions that express goals and ideals. Every institution of higher learning is built on a mission and a vision. The purpose of an institution's mission and vision is to create a common path for students and employees. Colleges focus on those ideals to direct everything from learning to co-curricular activities. While each institution must follow the mandates of the state in which it resides, it is this centering idea about learning that makes each school unique.

In Unit 1, we saw the Central Piedmont Community College vision statement. Haywood Community College's vision statement is: "Advancing our community through education and leadership." (Haywood Community College, 2012)

Write a 2-3 paragraph history of your college. Include when and why it began. How many students attend? You may also include some physical aspects of your college. How many campuses does your college have? What community organizations partner with your college? To what agencies and associations does your college belong? How many instructors work at your college? How large is your college in comparison to the other colleges in your state? What special awards or acknowledgements has your college achieved?

Use the following questions to prepare for the assignment above.

1. What is a Mission Statement? What is your college's Vision or Mission Statement?

2. What is a Vision Statement? What is your college's Vision Statement?

3. What is your college's motto, mascot or slogan? What is the history of that motto, mascot, or slogan?

COUNSELING AND ADVISING

Sometimes correctly placing the first step can determine if you will get where you want to go. Students take a lot of "first steps" as they try to make their way through the maze of services and resources available in college. College is a BIG first step. You will find that by talking to advisors and counselors, your fears, doubts, and questions will give way to a confident, positive action plan.

Here are some typical first steps for entry to college:

STEP 1 – Applying to college

"Take the first step in faith. You don't have to see the whole staircase, just take the first step." *---Martin Luther King, Jr.*

As a first step, colleges require potential students to fill out an application form. If you are reading this book, you have probably already done this, but you will fill out another form if you transfer, or if you apply to a program. The admissions process is different for every school and program. Some colleges have rigorous admissions requirements – grade point averages, testing, essays, and application information about you to ensure a good fit between students and the colleges' goals for student success and completion.

This is a good time to get a college catalog. The college catalog is a compilation of information about your college's history, degree programs, services for students and contact information for resources and departments. It will be useful as you focus your application and look at the next step.

What is the process for admission to your college?

How do you apply for admission?

STEP 2 – Requesting transcripts

"The first step binds one to the second." *---French proverb*

The next step in admission is providing documentation of your previous academic work. Enrolling in a college program usually requires submission of all relevant academic transcripts. Students are responsible for submitting their academic transcripts so that they can be efficiently processed for admission in a specific program.

At your college, what is the process to submit your academic transcripts?

STEP 3 – Testing

"A journey of a thousand miles begins with a single step." *---Lao Tzu*

Early in the admissions process, students usually take some type of placement test (or tests). The results of those tests determine proper placement in classes. Students should prepare for placement tests by reading all the information the college makes available about test logistics and format.

What is the process for placement testing at your college?

STEP 4 – Getting Help

"What saves a man is to take a step. Then another step." ---*Antoine de Saint-Exupery*

Meeting with an academic counselor or advisor is an important early step to take in the road to progress. Once you have completed Steps 1 – 3, you will want to make an appointment to talk to an advisor or counselor to determine your next steps. Often, after meeting with the counselor or advisor, you will declare a major or program of study.

If you are unsure about your program of study, you may be directed to a career counselor at your college. Career counselors help you define and accomplish your personal goals, explore career choices and help you understand the career development process.

If you are decided about your major, you may be directed to a faculty advisor who is well versed in the particular aspects of your major. The faculty advisor can help you develop, clarify, and evaluate your educational plans and goals, identify and explore alternatives, and look at the outcomes of your decisions.

If you have personal or health issues which may affect or influence your progress in college, you may also wish to speak to a personal counselor at your college. Counselors are caring professionals who can help you find solutions to some of the daily stresses and issues that students encounter as they begin this journey.

What is the counseling and advising process at your college?

What is the process for career counseling at your college?

What is the process for personal counseling at your college?

Many colleges offer these services online. Getting help from a website is accessible and convenient for students who are computer savvy. If, however, you are more comfortable with face-to-face discussions about your future, you can be sure that the counseling and advising services at your college have the time and caring professionals to make an appointment to see you in person.

Knowing how to access this information is essential.

Are online counseling and advising services available at your college?

What is the phone number and location of the counseling and advising office on your campus?

Once you have completed these first four steps and you have a potential list of classes to enroll in for the upcoming semester, it is time to register.

Student Voices: Carlos

Carlos had some friends who had a little experience taking classes at the community college. After listening to them discuss how *they* navigated through the system, Carlos assumed that he could skip a few steps and do it all on his own.

Several weeks later, when he had not heard back from the college, he assumed he had not been admitted. Struggling with a sense of failure and embarrassment, Carlos decided that maybe college was just not for him. While talking with his friends, Carlos discovered that they received information from the college in the official e-mail account assigned to them during the admissions process. Since he did not remember the information he had submitted during the online application process, he called the school's Help and Information telephone number and got his e-mail account access information.

Carlos found that he *had* been admitted and the semester would begin the following week. Because of the delay, his choices for classes were limited.

Disappointed, but relieved, Carlos met with an advisor to help him figure out which classes were best for his potential nursing career.

Carlos learned that making assumptions could dramatically alter his college career path. Since he had neither the time nor the money to waste, he decided he needed to be more engaged in the formal process of going to college.

Your Voice:

1. Why did Carlos skip steps?

2. What assumptions do students make about college processes?

3. What expectations did you have about college processes that were not met? How did you adjust your thinking to successfully get where you wanted to go?

Registration and your College Catalog*

Registering for classes is a process that is unique to each college. Critical information about dates and deadlines, payments, withdrawals, attendance and required grade point averages is often overlooked by students until it is too late.

The following exercises will help you review policies and procedures that can help you avoid missteps and practice setting up a schedule for the upcoming semester.

Using your college catalog or website, answer the following questions:

1. What are some different ways to register for courses at your college?

2. What is the tuition refund policy at your college?

3. What is the withdrawal policy at your college?

4. Other than attending classes on your current campus, what are two other ways to take courses at your college?

5. When are final exams during the current semester?

6. What is a Comprehensive Articulation Agreement?

7. At your college, which degrees are designed to transfer to other colleges?

8. How many credit hours do you need to complete your degree?

9. What are the definitions of "prerequisite" and "co requisite"?

10. According to your college catalog, what is the program grade-point average necessary to receive a degree, diploma, or certificate?

*Some colleges refer to the college catalog as the college bulletin.

Registration Exercise

Using the current course schedule, create a non-conflicting schedule for a new student who wants to take the following courses:

MAT 080

ENG 111

COM 110

CHM 090

For this exercise, you may only choose one online course for your schedule.

This student works on Mondays, Wednesdays, and Fridays from 10:00 a.m. to 3:00 p.m.

Course #	Section	Course Name	Day/Time	Campus
Ex: ACA 111	01	College Student Success	M/W 9:30 – 10:30	Central

Paying for College

Education is an investment in your future. Just like buying a house, most of us have to look for outside assistance to make the initial purchase. Filling out paperwork, completing on-line forms, or talking to a financial aid advisor are some of the college success skills that can make or break your ability to finish your degree. With a little work, a sensible plan, and focused determination, achieving your college goals becomes a realistic possibility.

The Financial Aid Department at your college can help you get started with the process of finding a way to pay for college. The staff can help you sort out the differences between loans, grants, and scholarships and show you where to look for the money you need to help pay for your classes, textbooks, lab fees, and other college-related expenses. Take time to investigate how the people in your college's financial aid office can help you look for alternative ways to pay for college.

College Costs

Attending classes, taking notes, and studying for tests are not the only responsibilities a student must take into account when preparing for college. Finding the money to pay for college can be an obstacle to a student's academic goals. In addition to tuition costs, there are lab, parking and activity fees to pay and expensive textbooks to purchase. You may also need to budget for transportation and child care. Students who live on campus must also take into account the cost of residence, meal plans and living expenses. Because costs vary from college to college and state to state, it's a good idea to determine how much money you will need.

Sample Costs:

2012–2013 Cost of Attendance at a Community College

Two term Budget	IN-STATE RESIDENTS		OUT-OF-STATE RESIDENTS	
	Not Living at Home/WO Parents Full-Time	Living at Home/WO Parents Full-Time	Not Living at Home/WO Parents Full-Time	Living at Home/WO Parents Full-Time
Tuition and Fees	$2,122	$2,122	$8,234	$8,234
Books and Supplies	$1,488	$1,488	$1,488	$1,488
Room and Board	$8,375	$4,188	$8,375	$4,188
Transportation	$4,509	$4,509	$4,509	$4,509
Misc.& Personal Expenses	$6,237	$6,237	$6,237	$6,237
TOTAL	$22,731	$18,544	$28,843	$24,656

(CPCC, 2012)

Use your college catalog (or website) to determine the costs of attendance for one academic year at your college.

Costs	In-State	Out-of-State
Tuition and Fees		
Books/Supplies		
Housing/Room		
Food		
Transportation		
Child Care		
Other		

Eligibility for Financial Aid

Many students make the mistake of thinking that financial aid is only for students whose income falls below the poverty level. This is not the case. Iin fact, some type of financial aid is available to most students.

To determine a student's eligibility for financial aid, their demonstrated financial need is calculated using the information on the previous year's tax returns. According to the U.S. Department of Education, "Need is the difference between the cost of education and what the parents and student might reasonably be expected to contribute to meet college costs" (U.S. Dept. Of Ed, 2012).

Students interested in obtaining federal financial aid need to complete the Free Application for Federal Student Aid, or FAFSA. This is the federal government form used to determine eligibility for federal financial aid.

What is federal government's official website for federal student aid?

Types of Financial Aid

The main types of financial aid are: Grants, loans, scholarships and work study.

A **grant** is a type of financial aid which does not have to be repaid. Eligibility for federal grants is based on financial need. The largest grant is the Federal Pell Grant and there are also other federal and state grants available to students.

Students who do not qualify for grants due to their income level may be eligible for a **student loan**. The benefits of a student loan include a lower interest rate than a personal bank loan, and a deferred payment date of six months after the date of college graduation. Students who qualify for loans will often be awarded more money than they need. They should only accept what they need to pay for college expenses. Remember, the amount you borrow is the amount you pay back.

You may see students from your classes working at the college. They are probably part of a federal **work-study** program designed to provide eligible students with an on campus part-time job. These positions are generally need-based.

Scholarships are often overlooked by students who believe that they do not have what it takes to earn them. There are two main categories of scholarships: merit based and need based. The term need-based refers to qualification based on the student's financial need. Merit-based scholarships are those that are earned through academic excellence, athletic ability, talent, community service, or some other social criterion. For example, there are scholarships available for left handed students, vegetarians, or children of U.S. veterans.

Although many national scholarships are competitive and open to thousands of applicants, there are also local scholarships with much smaller applicant pools. Do not make the mistake of thinking that you may not be eligible for any scholarships. According to College Board, "In general, the smaller the geographic area a scholarship covers, the better the student's chances of winning" (College Board, 2012).

Several helpful sources for scholarships include: local and state agencies, your college or university, scholarship websites, and the Department of Education website at: www.federalstudentaid.ed.gov/scholarship.

Getting Started

Visit your college's Financial Aid office, or the official Department of Education website to begin the process of paying for college. The earlier you apply the better. In fact, students may begin applying as early as January for the upcoming fall semester. It is never too late to get started!

Jakilya Hood

Paying for College: Accessing Financial Aid Resources at your college

1. Where is the financial aid office located on your college campus?

    Central high 206   704-330-6942

2. What is your college's financial aid website?

    cpp.edu / Financial aid

3. What application is required in order to be considered for federal financial aid?

    FAFSA

4. How do students demonstrate their financial need? Which documents are required?   Taxes

5. List three types of financial aid available to college students.

    : grant
    . student loans
    : grants

6. When is the earliest you can apply for financial aid, and why?

    ~~are due date~~ Jan. 1st

7. What is one benefit of obtaining a federal student loan versus a private bank loan?   lower interest rate, differed intrest rate

8. What is a Federal Pell Grant, and how is eligibility determined?

    Federal money that they give you to go to school but you have to work to keep it

9. What is the difference between a merit-based scholarship and a need-based scholarship?   Merit is based on grades and need based is based on financial need

10. List two local scholarships for which you are eligible. (Hint: Check your college website, local agencies, and the US Department of Education website.)

    Library scholarship

Library Services

Welcome to the new library. If you have not been in a library for a while, you are in for a big surprise. The library still has lots of books, but it also has electronic and media resources paired with an energetic and knowledgeable staff to help you with your information search. To take full advantage of all library services, you will need to know a few facts about the library at your college.

Computer Technology

Because everything in the library is now computerized, you will have to be computer savvy to take full advantage of all its services. There is an exercise at the end of this section to help you learn how to navigate the library site.

Accessibility of Services

Many colleges have a central campus and several branch or satellite campuses throughout the community. What you may not know is that each of those campuses generally has a fully functional library offering complete services. This is made possible through the use of computer technology. You will be able to access library services from computers at work, home, or another library using your college ID.

The Energetic and Knowledgeable Staff

Librarians may well be the library's most underutilized resource. Every campus library is staffed with professional and friendly librarians whose job it is to help you find what you are researching. Although it may seem as though they are always busy working on something, they are actually there to answer your questions. Librarians pride themselves on being familiar with ever-changing streams of information flow. To keep abreast of everything that is going on, the librarians are constantly researching, exploring, and sampling. Do not hesitate to ask for help. The choice is yours. You can waste time trying to find it yourself, or you can ask for assistance and drastically reduce the time spent looking for information. Through the use of computer technology you can often get librarian assistance from home, work, and even after regular library hours. The librarians are here for you. Use them!

Library Myths or Facts...Sleuth the Stacks

The following statements are common beliefs about the library. Research your library and discover the truth.

Are the following statements True or False? *Explain your answers.*

1. Everyone who works in the library is a librarian. They are all older women who wear glasses and are very old-fashioned.

2. The information on the internet is just as good as what is on the library databases.

3. The internet will soon make libraries obsolete.

4. The library is only for smart people.

5. The library is boring.

6. You cannot eat or drink in the library, so it is difficult to work for long periods of time there.

7. Librarians read all the time.

8. Talking is forbidden in the library.

9. Using the library is just another way for the government to keep track of you.

10. If you lose a book from the library, you will not be able to graduate.

Campus Security

A college campus is a very open and accessible environment. Therefore, the services of Campus Security are provided for your safety. There are students, faculty, staff, administrators and visitors on campus at any time. Campus security personnel are employed on college campuses to ensure that everyone has a safe and non-threatening environment in which to pursue his or her academic endeavors.

Personal Safety
Your personal safety is of utmost importance to Campus Security. Many college campuses are open to the public, and it can sometimes be difficult to identify who is a student and who is not. For that reason it is important that you obtain a college identification card (ID) and carry it throughout the semester.

It is advisable to keep personal belongings with you at all times. Campus libraries, restrooms, and classrooms are prime target areas for thieves. Do not leave textbooks, electronic devices and personal items unattended while on campus.   If you lose an item, check your campus Lost and Found. If you believe that an item has been stolen, contact campus security immediately to report the incident. And, if you find an unattended item, you should report it to Campus Security at once.

Security personnel at most colleges will provide students with escorts to their vehicles or to classes in the evenings. There is no need to walk to your car alone. If you feel uncomfortable walking to class or to a parking lot, contact security personnel on your campus to ask for an escort.

Parking Safety
One of the major responsibilities of Campus Security is parking safety. Students who use campus parking need to know and comply with the parking regulations at their college. Most colleges provide students with a parking sticker once their car has been registered with campus security or parking services. Be sure to display your sticker at all times to prevent avoidable ticketing.

Students must take precautions to lock their cars and to keep valuables with them at all times. Leaving valuables in your car in plain view may result in a broken window and stolen property.   Follow this rule: If you do not need it, leave it at home. It is imperative that you report any incidents to Campus Security, no matter how insignificant the incident may seem.

Discriminatory and Sexual Harassment
A growing area of concern for campus security is harassment. Harassment is defined as any action from one person to another that is unwanted or seen as threatening. All college students, faculty, and staff have the right to function in a mature, respectful, and adult environment. Report all incidents of harassment to the appropriate authority.

Refer to your college's security website to answer these questions.

1. Where is the Lost and Found located on your campus?

2. What is the emergency phone number for campus security on your college campus?

3. What is the non-emergency phone number for campus security?

4. Does your college campus provide emergency phones on campus or in the parking lots? If so, where are they located?

Campus Security Exercise

What Do I Do Now?

Read each scenario and comment on what you would do next.

1. You have dialed the campus emergency phone number for a student with a medical emergency. When the dispatcher answers you should:

2. While in class, you have been informed by your instructor that an emergency situation has occurred on campus and all students, faculty and staff are in a lockdown.

3. As you are walking to class, you notice something that appears to be blood on the floor in the hallway.

4. A student from one of your classes sends e-mails to you about non-school related topics. You have been polite and ignored the emails, but you continue to be contacted. Eventually, the e-mails become more suggestive and you are uncomfortable with them.

5. You are in the parking lot, preparing to leave for the day when you witness someone backing their car into a parked car on campus and driving away.

6. You return to your car in the parking lot to find that someone has been in your car. You may have forgotten to lock it. Nothing is stolen, but there is evidence that someone has been in your car.

Technology and Student Success

If you think you are technologically adept, you may need a reality check. Knowing how to upload photos on Facebook, follow a discussion on Twitter and use Google to search for information are great skills to possess. But what does it mean to master technology in a college setting?

Educational technology is designed to enhance your college experience, and it is constantly changing and improving. Are you prepared for the challenge of using the latest technology resources in college?

According to McKeachie (2011), college technology tools can be grouped into four categories:

- Communication
- Presentation
- Information Searching and Resource Management
- Course Management Systems

As a college student, you will need to become familiar with technology related tasks in all of the areas listed above. Whether you are emailing an instructor about an assignment, responding to a fellow student's online discussion board post or receiving a college-wide text alert about an inclement weather class cancellation, technology will play a role.

Communication with instructors

Did you know that email is the best way to contact most college instructors? Although your instructors have offices and phones, contacting instructors through your college email ensures that they recognize your message as one sent by an official or currently enrolled student. It also provides an email trail that allows you to track the communication.

Instructor-student communication can be a key to success in a course. College email accounts are accessible tools for students who may have questions about coursework or grades, and do not have time to visit the instructor in person. In addition, instructors can communicate with students individually or as an entire class, and can inform them of any updates, provide feedback on coursework, or even relay information about class cancellations or relocations. Checking your email can prevent you from missing a class that was moved or showing up for a class that has been cancelled.

A common misconception among college students is that instructors will, and should, reply to emails instantaneously. The truth is that each instructor has different guidelines for responding to students, and it is up to the student to learn those guidelines.

Knowing your college instructors' expectations and knowing how to access technology resources at your college are ways to ensure that you are technologically prepared for college.

Essential Technology Skills:

- ability to type, and to save and attach documents
- ability to access and professionally use college email accounts
- ability to access your college's Information Technology (IT) services/helpdesk
- ability to use the college's learning management system (Blackboard, WebCT)
- ability to access computers and labs, the internet, and printers on campus
- use of Netiquette
- compliance with your college's computer use policies and procedures

---

Technology and online classes

As part of your college experience, you will have the option of taking certain classes in a fully online format. Knowing how to use technology to access course information and to submit assignments online is a key to your success in *all* classes, but especially in online classes.

Online classes are generally housed in a Learning Management System (LMS) such as Blackboard. As an online student, you will be responsible for accessing course materials, submitting course work online, checking grades, participating in online discussions and communicating with the instructor and your classmates. All of that, in addition to your course work, can be a daunting task. Be sure to find out if your college offers an orientation to e-learning (or distance learning), and take advantage of it. Be prepared to fulfill a wide range of tasks in your online course.

Using technology to navigate college resources

Technology is not just for communication and course work. In fact, more and more students are both searching for courses and registering for them online. College websites have made it easy to access course offerings, college catalogs, exam schedules and program or degree evaluations online. It is to your advantage to know how to navigate your college's website and its online services and resources.

Technology Security

For your security, it would be wise to adhere to the following tips about computer usage:

1. Do not write down your username and password together. If anyone gains access to both your username and password, he or she can assume your identity to sign on to any computer.

2. Remember to log off the computer when you are finished using it. If you do not log off the computer, the next user has access to your login and can run programs, print documents and send email under your name.

3. Only currently enrolled students are allowed access to campus computers. Do not share your username and password with friends or relatives.

4. Technology services at your school exist to help you with problems that you may experience while using computing services. Do not hesitate to call with questions.

Accessing Your College's Technology Resources

1. What is the process for activating your student email account?

2. Should you use your personal e-mail account to communicate with instructors?

3. Where are student computer labs located on your campus? What are the requirements for using them?

4. Once you create a password, is it secure? How will you know?

5. If you forget your log-in or password, what should you do?

6. If you need assistance to log in or to access technology services, who do you call?

7. Which Learning Management System (LMS) is used at your college? How can you receive an orientation or training to use that system?

8. How do you find out if you have a printing account for campus printers?

9. What are your instructor's expectations for the use of technology (laptops, iPads, cell phones) in the classroom?

10. What is the proper netiquette salutation to address an instructor or administrator in an e-mail?

Tutoring and Academic Assistance

As a college student, you may find that the road to success is not always easy, and that you have difficulty achieving good grades in all your classes.

Does this sound like you?

- I just received a failing grade on a math test.
- I am having difficulty comprehending course content and lecture material in economics.
- My English professor has referred me to a writing center to get help to revise an essay.
- My GPA is low and I have been placed on academic warning.
- I could use some help with grammar and writing skills.
- I need help preparing for a biology exam.
- Foreign languages are not my thing and I could use some help with my Spanish class.
- I would really like to improve my study skills and take better notes in class.
- I don't need any help. I got through high school just fine.

If you have been in any of the situations listed above, then it may be time to visit your college's academic assistance or tutoring center. Most colleges offer academic assistance in the form of tutoring, workshops and assessments to help students overcome difficulties with academic coursework.

Tutoring services are often available to college students in various forms: one-on-one, online, group and peer tutoring. Most tutors are required to have experience and success in the courses in which they tutor. They are qualified to help you achieve success in your courses.

Academic assistance is available to college students in other forms, as well. Most colleges offer workshops related to study skills, test anxiety and time management. Students can also receive help preparing for placement tests and other standardized tests. Some colleges offer personalized learning styles assessments to assist students in finding study skills which best suit their learning style.

The good news is that these services are usually offered at no charge to currently enrolled college students. It is up to you to take advantage of them.

Student Voices: LaTonya

We learned in Unit 1 that LaTonya found certain subjects to be easier than others. Learning history, English or other lecture-based subjects was a challenge for LaTonya, but classes such as math and science were easier, and seemed to be a better fit.

Her preference for visual learning was key to understanding how she learned best, and to determining how to approach studying, note taking and test taking. LaTonya found it helpful when professors and instructors provided handouts, power point slides or notes on the board. But there was still a missing piece. LaTonya's writing skills were not where she needed them to be in order for her to achieve the A's she wanted in her required English classes.

During the fall semester, LaTonya's English Composition instructor returned a graded midterm essay, and included a note recommending that LaTonya meet with a writing tutor to further refine her essay.   LaTonya's only previous interaction with a tutor had been in elementary school, when she had to stay after school each week to receive help with reading. It had not been a positive experience, and the current referral for tutoring felt like punishment.

LaTonya realized it was time to put her past perceptions aside and take advantage of the services her college had to offer. The English grade needed to improve, and she decided to take action.

LaTonya found her campus Academic Assistance and Tutoring Center, and learned that walk-in appointments were accepted. That made the center accessible and convenient for her. She met with the writing tutor to review her essay. They planned revisions and scheduled a second appointment to review the results. The tutor also showed LaTonya how to access assistance online.

Your voice:

- Why was LaTonya reluctant to receive tutoring?

- What type of tutoring assistance is available at your college?

- How would you benefit from receiving academic assistance?

TUTORING AND ACADEMIC ASSISTANCE SERVICES AT YOUR COLLEGE

The following questions will better prepare you to get the most out of your academic assistance and tutoring experience. Investigating these services at your college will allow you to be prepared when it is time to use them.

1. Where is the academic assistance or tutoring center located on your campus?

2. Do you need a referral?

3. If available, what is the process for accessing academic assistance online at your college?

4. What types of tutoring are offered? In- person, online, group?

5. Do you need to schedule an appointment, or can you "drop in"?

6. What are the hours/days of operation for the academic assistance or tutoring center on your campus?

7. For which subjects is tutoring offered?

8. What are the credentials of the tutors?

9. What types of tutoring assistance are you most likely to need?

10. What other types of assistance are available to students at the center?

Policies and Procedures

Colleges as Bureaucracies

The word "bureaucracy" has a negative association for most people. The sociologist Max Weber, however, saw modern systems of bureaucracy as advances in efficiencies over older methods of organization—yes, bureaucracies *improve* efficiencies. At least, they improve the efficient accomplishment of the specific task they are designed to accomplish. Unfortunately, sometimes a badly designed system never fits the needs it was supposed to fulfill, and sometimes the needs change so that the system is no longer efficient.

Of course, there are times when we do not want too much efficiency. For the student who has not registered for class by the end of the registration period, the registration period *itself* may seem to be an artificial bureaucratic barrier to getting what he or she wants. That student fails to recognize that the registration process was the most efficient means to register the thousands of students who got classes. North Carolina community colleges serve more than 800,000 students every year (Public Affairs, 2011). Inconvenience for 8,000 is convenience for 792,000.

A well-designed bureaucratic system has certain characteristics:

1. Formal hierarchy

2. Management by clear-cut (written) rules

3. Clear division of labor with specific assignments

4. Hiring and promotion by technical competence (rather than personal favoritism)

5. Calculability of results appropriate to specific jurisdictional area

6. Career paths in which people are protected from arbitrary rule changes.

You may be able to imagine how this applies to a college.

1. Students, teachers, department heads, deans, vice presidents, and presidents form a hierarchy.

2. Each is governed by rules "appropriate" to their level in the hierarchy. Students, for example, pay to go to class. There is a tuition rule. Teachers are paid to go to class. There is a payment rule.

3. Each level of the school has specific jobs. Students, teachers, and administrators all have roles specific to their position in the system.

4. People are hired to teach according to their demonstrated competencies in a disciplinary area. In the United States, instructors teaching college-level academic classes are generally required to have a Master's degree and at least 18 credits of graduate-level work in the areas in which they are teaching. It does not matter how personable or popular they are, if they do not have those credentials, they are not permitted to teach.

5. Calculation is also appropriate to each level of the hierarchy. Students, teachers, and administrators all determine resources and results as appropriate to their level in the hierarchy. Students, for example, are interested in costs and grades. Instructors may be interested in grades and completions.

6. For students, one of the most important of those bureaucratic characteristics is the last one: the "career path". When you declare your major you are matriculated into a catalog year and are bound to that catalog. Your college catalog outlines your path toward graduation. If the college changes the rules for graduation, those new rules do not apply to you as long as you are covered by your catalog. For that reason, most colleges have a maximum time that a student can remain under the jurisdiction of their catalog.

Policies and Procedures

College catalogs outline the rules of the bureaucracy you are entering. Colleges use bureaucratic systems to ensure the safety and the fair treatment of all students, faculty, and staff. Colleges codify well-established procedures developed through years of experience in a set of policies and procedures. Those are the "written rules" under which college life and work is managed. Most colleges set aside the procedures that apply most directly to students as a student handbook. You might think of it as an operator's manual for college.

Like an operator's manual for a car, a student handbook can serve as your survival kit to help you when something unexpected arises in your college career. At some point in college, all students encounter some problem, worry, or disruption. That is when the student handbook comes in handiest. Handbooks typically have information about policies and procedures to inform you of your rights as a student, about campus resources and tips on how to use them, references to campus activities and programs, and much more. As a part of the "rights and responsibility" section, student handbooks contain grading and disciplinary regulations, including students' rights and responsibilities.

At some schools, the student handbook narrowly concentrates on those essential rights, responsibilities, and regulations. At other schools, the student handbook is a condensed version of the college catalog, and covers the rights, responsibilities, and regulations, as well as references to student services.

In all cases, however, the handbook has a wealth of information that is essential when students most need it. It is always a good idea to know where the handbook is, and to become familiar with it before any problems arise. Often, that prior knowledge can allow you to avoid problems.

For example, student handbooks cover regulations about plagiarism. Instructors enforce those regulations as they are outlined in the student handbook. Usually, there really is only one plagiarism policy at any college. It is stressed differently in various classes, but the policy is outlined in the student handbook. Students who follow the regulations as written in the student handbook generally do not have to worry about committing plagiarism.

Because student handbooks also outline the technical procedures by which discipline is administered, they also outline the procedures students can use to ensure they are treated fairly. In the plagiarism example, instructors can only impose penalties specified for violation of the student code of conduct. In most schools, that policy would come under academic integrity. Academic integrity policies at most schools permit expulsion for plagiarism. If the most severe penalty at your school is course failure, then expulsion is not a listed penalty. An instructor would be mistaken to threaten expulsion if course failure were the most severe penalty permitted under policies and procedures.

The best way to learn about the student handbook is to use it. Your instructor may assign an exercise in this course to help you to become more familiar with the student handbook.

Student Voices: Kyle

Kyle was in his psychology class. Before class began, he had been using his phone to check on and update a couple of his social media accounts. He knew that his psychology teacher was a real stickler for the rules, and she had said that no one was allowed to use cell phones in class. There was even something about it in the syllabus. Kyle was waiting for a reply to an information request he had posted, and so he left his phone on the desk so he would see the reply when it came in. When class began, Dr. Avery looked over at Kyle and told him to put his phone away. Kyle said he was not using his phone. Dr. Avery just looked at him, and so Kyle moved his phone into his backpack, but where it was still visible. Kyle checked on his phone occasionally as the class discussed a chemical reaction that was supposed to be responsible for mood shifts. Unfortunately, Kyle used an MP3 of an old fashioned electric typewriter as his social media notification sound. When he got his reply, Kyle's backpack started emitting the loud, clacking of  a typewriter. Dr. Avery was livid. She walked to the door, and told Kyle to gather his belongings and join her in the hall. He tried to argue, but she stood unmoved. When they got to the hall, Kyle apologized again, but Dr. Avery said he would be hearing from the Dean.

That afternoon, Kyle got an email from the Dean requesting a meeting the next day. The email was very scary. It said Kyle was charged with a violation of the *College Electronic Devices Policy*, Section IV. A. 5b, *Disruption*, Section IV. A. 2c, and *Failure to Comply*, Section IV. A. 2e. The email also said that Kyle was not allowed to return to class until the issue was resolved.

At this point, Kyle suspected he might be in trouble. He had no idea what to do.

Your Voice:

1. What cues about class policies did Kyle ignore?

2. At your school, are there general electronic device (cell phone) polices? What does your Student Handbook say about general rules such as the "failure to comply" regulation that Kyle violated?

3. Do you ever use a cell phone in class? At your school, what penalties do you face for using a cell phone?

Student Handbook Worksheet

Directions: Prepare an oral presentation about one of the policies and procedures in your Student Handbook. Select your topic from the list below and tell your instructor the topic you have chosen. During your presentation, you should explain your particular topic and give an example of how to utilize the policy or procedure. The following worksheet will help you to design your presentation. To prepare your presentation, you must refer to and cite your Handbook, Catalog, or Policies and Procedures Manual.

Presentation Topics

Select one topic from the following choices. Discuss your choice with your instructor.

_____ Definitions under the student academic integrity policy

_____ General regulations and appeal process of student academic integrity policy

_____ Grading policies (grade assignments)

_____ Grading policies (grade troubles through auditing courses)

_____ Grading policies (academic honors)

_____ Student grievance procedure

_____ Student code of conduct

_____ Disciplinary procedures

_____ Appeals procedure

_____ Confidentiality of student records

_____ Changing grades (see Policies and Procedures manual)

_____ Graduation (see Policies and Procedures manual)

Diversity

One of the reasons there is so much emphasis on policies and procedures is the sheer scale and diversity in college populations. Because of that scale, colleges need standardized operating procedures to prevent personal biases from making college arbitrary and unpredictable.

When you think of large-scale systems, the military or the federal government may come to mind. Combined U.S. military forces in September, 2009 comprised 1.2 million (Dept. of Defense, 2009). Total federal employment that year was 2.3 million (Bureau of Labor Statistics, 2010). In contrast, more than 20.4 million people enrolled in colleges in the United States in the fall of 2009 (National Center for Educational statistics, 2010). Only California and Texas would have larger populations than the Great State of College.

In the North Carolina Community College system, only 29% of the student population fall in the "typical" student age range (18-24) for comparison, that age range comprised nearly 85% of the UNC System student population (Duda, 2008). Nationwide, however, increasing numbers of 18-24 year old students have been enrolling in community colleges (Mullin, 2012), and that age group now comprises nearly 53 percent of community college students. Younger students enrolled in community colleges, however, are still different than their university counterparts. University students are much more likely to identify primarily as students, while community college students more frequently think of themselves as primarily part of the workforce. They are also more likely to be part-time students, and are far more likely to work more than 20 hours a week. As we see this national shift toward younger students, we can also see the future of the United States reflected in student populations.

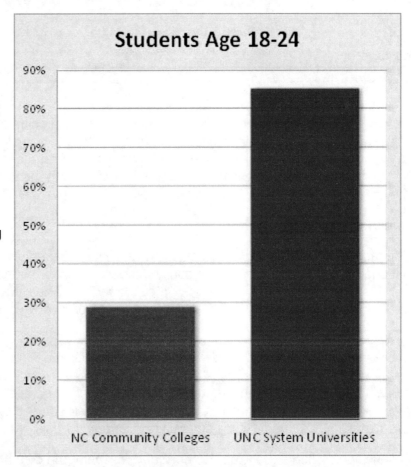

Those 20 million college students are as diverse as the world in which they live. Keeping in mind that different schools have vastly different demographics, it is still a safe bet that college demographics are generally much more diverse than the smaller networks of friends and family with whom we spend most of our time. The diversity in higher education is expected to continue to reflect the increasingly diverse demographics of the United States.

Table 3.3

**Number of U.S. College Students and Projected Change 2010-2018,
by Race and Hispanic Origin**

	Number of students				Percent Increase over 2010		
	2010	2011	2014	2018	2011	2014	2018
American Indian	219,896	223,361	234,267	250,769	2%	7%	14%
Asian and Pacific Islander	1,292,297	1,324,153	1,433,709	1,568,436	2%	11%	21%
Black non-Hispanic	2,506,594	2,560,579	2,778,311	2,995,165	2%	11%	19%
Hispanic	2,259,427	2,324,158	2,568,116	2,863,277	3%	14%	27%
White non-Hispanic	12,181,946	12,182,495	12,226,032	12,228,388	0	0	0
Nonresident foreign	665,620	671,196	687,324	714,197	1%	3%	7%

Source: Baum, Sandy. 2011

In Table 3.3, we see projected changes in the diversity of college students in the United States. In 2010, 64% of all college students were "White, non-Hispanic" (Hispanics can be of any race, and this study assigned all Hispanics to the category, "Hispanic"). Although the *number* of white non-Hispanic students is projected to increase slightly through 2018, they will only constitute 59% of all students.

Racial Diversity:

The racial and ethnic composition of North Carolina Community Colleges mirrors closely the national trends in those areas. Nationally, 68 percent of community college students were non-Hispanic Whites, and 38 percent African American, Asian, Native American, or Hispanics of any race (Mullin, 2012). In North Carolina, those percentages were 64% and 36%, respectively (Duda, 2008).

Because younger segments of the population in the United States are more diverse than older segments of the population, most community colleges serve a higher percentage of minority students than would be represented by the population in general. They accurately reflect the racial and ethnic composition of the population in their student age groups. In North Carolina, this pattern holds true in at the smallest and largest schools. Roanoke-Chowan Community

College serves Bertie, Chowan, Hertford and Northampton counties in the northeast part of the state. The population of those counties is 58% racial and ethnic minorities, while the college is 68% minorities. Central Piedmont Community College in Charlotte serves Mecklenburg County. The county is 34% minority, while the college is 43% minority (Duda, 2008). Recent high school graduates will find community college populations similar to the population of the school systems from which they graduated. Older students may be surprised by the diversity.

Critical Thinking About the Data

The discussion of racial diversity suggests a possible reason for the patterns of minority enrollment that are projected in Table 3.1.

1. What is the reason suggested in the text?

2. What are some other reasons you can think of?

International Diversity

In this increasingly global economy, many employers want students to think of themselves as preparing to join an international workforce (Hart, 2006). Many community colleges and most four year colleges and universities enroll students from around the world. The number of international students peaked in 2008-2009 (Fischer, 2009), but still accounts for nearly five percent of total college enrollment in the United States. Most colleges and universities also maintain study abroad programs, and some colleges maintain international degree programs, in which students and faculty work and study in two or more countries. Almost all colleges, however, have some form of international study or international interest clubs--sometimes organized around language departments, and usually supported by Student Life.

International students in the United States are unevenly distributed, of course, with some colleges having large numbers and other colleges hosting relatively few international students. In either case, a well-rounded college education introduces native students to their international counterparts, and vice versa.

NAFSA: the Association of International Educators tracks the annual economic impact of international students, and they estimated that international students and their families contributed more than $20 billion to the US economy. In 2011, North Carolina schools reported 12,824 international students enrolled under F-1 or M-1 Student Visas (NAFSA, 2012). Not surprisingly, most of these international students attend the large universities, but they attend schools all over the state. Interestingly, 3,235 international students attended North Carolina State University, which was nearly twice the number that attended the University of North Carolina. Of the big state universities, the University of North Carolina Charlotte came in third with 1,300 students. Duke University and Medical Center enrolled 2,485 international students. Wake Forest University, Eastern Carolina University, Central Piedmont Community College, and Wake Technical College all had roughly the same number of international students--between 300 and 320 (NAFSA, 2012).

For each of the comments on the left, find the appropriate answer on the right

1) Why might International students be concentrated at schools like North Carolina State, North Carolina A & T, and Duke?

2) Why would international students be as likely to attend private colleges as they would be to attend state colleges and universities?

3) Why is minority enrollment at most community colleges higher than the minority population percentage in the surrounding communities?

4) How are policies and procedures related to diversity?

5) In terms of future employment, why would it be a good idea to make yourself aware of the international diversity of your college?

6) In terms of expanding educational opportunities, why would it be a good idea to make yourself aware of the international diversity of your college?

7) The text book says that community college students are starting to reflect a younger segment of the population. What sort of diversity might you lose if that trend continues?

a) International students often concentrate in IT, engineering, agricultural and medical, programs. Agriculture and engineering programs are often concentrated in land-grant universities.

b) International students pay out-of-state tuition and are ineligible for financial aid, lowering the cost advantage of state schools.

c) There are more minorities in college-age population than in the over-all population.

d) Formal policies and procedures ensure everyone is treated the same.

e) Employers are looking for international awareness; stressing the international diversity of your education is an easy way to develop and demonstrate that awareness.

f) International educational opportunities may be sitting next to you. Talking with classmates is often good way to find out about other countries.

g) With a more uniformly young population, the opportunity to learn with a diverse age group is lost. Students who want that experience must actively seek those learning opportunities

Opportunities in Diversity

Does your college environment reflect the world in which you live outside of college? What opportunities does your college provide to prepare you for the global economy? Most students discover that their college classroom is the most diverse setting in their daily lives: it contains a wide range of ages, of racial, ethnic, and national origin backgrounds. It would be unfortunate to get through school without taking the opportunity to discover the world that is all around you.

Student Voices: Tom

Tom was open to the idea of taking a communication class. After all, he would have to communicate with customers at his restaurant someday. He did not like sitting through other students' presentations, even though a lot of them were about food. On the bright side, his classmates often brought samples of some food item that they liked. Most of his classmates knew about eating food, or knew simple recipes, but nothing that really connected to Tom's professional interest. One of his classmates, Shilpi, gave a presentation on vegetarian cuisine, and Tom knew he was not interested in learning vegetarian cooking.

Shilpi was from India, and brought home-made Samosas (a potato stuffed pastry) for the class to try. Tom had been to an Indian restaurant once. He did not understand the cuisine, and never thought about the experience afterward, even when he later became interesting in cooking. Shilpi's samosas were a revelation. The potatoes retained their texture and seemed infused with a wonderful flavor that he could not identify. There were green peas that almost tasted like lentils. Most amazing, though, there was a sharp, biting spiciness that was like a chili, but that did not seem to have any chili taste. Tom asked Shilpi about it, and she said that that flavor he could not identify was a *garam masala* that her mother ground from seeds. She could not explain the rest of the dish.

Tom left class and went to the library, where he looked up the recipe for Samosas. There were two kinds of chilis in the dish, and it turned out garam masala meant "hot spice mixture," and it was made of at least 10 different spices mixed together according to the cook's taste.

He started thinking that he had been approaching spices wrong. Instead of shaking spices from a can, maybe he should make his own spice mixtures. If there was a balance of chilis and spices that would take away the chili flavor and retain the chili spiciness, then maybe he could isolate other flavors as well.

Your Voice

1. What about Tom's attitude going into the presentations might have kept him from learning from Shilpi and the other students in the class?

2. Do your instructors try to get students to share their insights?

3. What could you do to be open to the informal curriculum your classmates offer?

Who is in your classroom? Activity

Find in your classes students who represent the sorts of diversity discussed in this section: age, national origin, race, and ethnicity. Find and interview students who you think may be different than you in terms of age, race, ethnicity, and national origin. Ask them why they are in school, and why they are in *this* school. Ask them the sorts of questions you are learning to answer about yourself. Your instructor may provide more detailed instructions.

College Career Connection

In 2011 the Chicago Press published a book entitled *Academically Adrift*. The book asks the question "How much are students actually learning in contemporary higher education?" Unfortunately, authors Richard Arum, professor of sociology and education at New York University, and Josipa Roksa, assistant professor of sociology at the University of Virginia concluded "not much" (2011). They cite data taken from the Collegiate Learning Assessment (2012) which is a standardized test taken by first semester freshmen and readministered at the end of their sophomore year. The results show that almost half of college students did not demonstrate any significant increase in learning skills (critical thinking, complex reasoning, and writing) within this time period. These results point to the sorts of problems that have led employers, colleges, and students to question the value of a college education.

Employers have begun to ask a series of questions about the quality of education that their future employees are receiving.

1. What are students learning and how will they use this knowledge in the workplace?
2. Other than course content, what are students learning that will help them survive and thrive in the workforce?
3. Are students learning the skills that they will need to become effective and productive employees or business owners?
4. What evidence can be presented to demonstrate student learning?

To answer these questions and concerns, colleges increasingly use assessments other than grades and are teaching skills beyond course content. "Institutional effectiveness" teams are searching for ways to document student learning. Colleges have adopted a set of common standards to provide evidence of student learning. Core abilities, competencies, values, and "common core" are a few of the terms used to define these initiatives. These standards are identified in each course and are meant to enhance student learning. They translate into skills necessary to secure employment in this competitive workforce. In addition, these standards are also infused into extracurricular activities to provide students learning opportunities both inside and outside of the classroom.

- What are the common skills that are incorporated in your college's courses?

Students increasingly question the value of their degree in the job market. As students reach the end of their college career and prepare to enter the job market, many students realize they should have been thinking about this when they first started college. They may be pressured by looming student loan repayments and fierce competition for limited employment opportunities. Many students have found that the best advantage they have is a well-rounded resume that boasts of not only academic achievement (good grades), but evidence of learning. They find that they also need to show evidence of employable skills such as: communication, critical thinking, self-management, global perspectives, quantitative literacy, civic engagement, and leadership. As you select courses to complete your degree, you should identify and keep track of these skills as they will prove to be a vital part of your resume.

In addition to documentation of what you have learned and the skills you have acquired, there are other things that your college offers that will enhance your resume. In most colleges, student organizations and activities are coordinated by a student life area. You will find that student life offers many of these opportunities.

Student Life

The process of learning requires more than listening to lectures, writing papers, doing projects, and completing computer assignments. Extracurricular activities enhance and add value to the content learned in coursework. In addition, these activities can help students develop social skills that will be necessary for survival in the workplace and provide the opportunity to document those skills. These skills include teamwork, leadership, and civic engagement.

Teamwork

Teamwork is defined as "the process of working collaboratively with a group of people in order to achieve a goal" (Business Dictionary, 2012). Teamwork is a vital part of every business and an essential skill that employers look for in potential employees. In college, students have numerous opportunities to develop their teamwork skills. The best opportunities are found in student clubs and organizations. Clubs and organizations fall into four categories:

1. Academic clubs often focus on an academic area, but also include general honor societies.
2. Social clubs include fraternities, sororities, and service organizations.
3. Athletic clubs include intermural and club sports.
4. Special interest clubs include religious, cultural, and other interest areas.

You are sure to find at least one club or organization that appeals to you. If you cannot find one, maybe you can start one.

Leadership and Student Government

Colleges offer opportunities for student leadership in the form of student government, leadership programs, and training. Students graduate every year, so a new crop of leaders is always emerging. Student government provides opportunities to engage in strategic planning, manage budgets, and represent the entire student population. In most colleges, the Student Government Association president sits as a non-voting member of the College Cabinet. Getting involved with student government builds leadership skills and offers experiences and references that you can include on your resume.

Civic Engagement

For many colleges, civic engagement is not just an option; it is a requirement. Civic engagement is a great way to enhance learning in your courses, give back to the community, and meet some interesting new people. Service Learning is a civic engagement model that combines community service with instruction and reflection. These programs enrich the learning experience by teaching civic responsibility while improving and strengthening communities.

Getting involved in extracurricular activities at your college will help you to make connections with your instructors, college staff and administration, and other students. You will begin to feel more like a college student, and not like someone who is just taking a bunch of classes. More importantly, you will have the opportunity to meet new people and build friendships that can last a lifetime.

Student Voices: Renee

School does not come easy for Renee. She has always been an average "C" student. She knows, however, that without a college degree she will not have as many opportunities for jobs and careers as those who hold a college degree. Renee's high school counselor recommended she begin her college career by attending the local community college to complete her general education requirements. She would then have the option to transfer to a college or university, or to complete her associate's degree and begin her career.

The community college was nothing like Renee imagined it would be. When she walked across the campus, instead of overhearing stimulating intellectual conversations about current events, she overheard discussions about the best day-care centers or where to get a good part-time job. She really did not feel connected to her fellow classmates-they just came to class and left immediately to go to work or to go home.

One day at the end of class, one of her classmates asked Renee if she planned to attend something called "Student Resources Day" in the quad. She had no idea what he was talking about, but she decided to check it out. Renee was amazed at what she found – student clubs, organizations, support services, and more. She spent an entire hour walking through the exhibits and talking to the representatives. She even ran into a few students from her classes. Renee felt much better now. She collected a dozen or so information sheets and brochures and went home to discuss her new options with her parents.

Your Voice:

1. Why did Renee not feel a connection with her classmates or instructors?

2. How can you get more connected with your classmates and instructors?

3. What are some of the clubs and organizations that interest you at your college?

Unit 4
It's About
Your Future

It's About Your Future

You have made the first step. You are on your way. This is not to say that those who did not decide to go to college are going nowhere, but a college degree will give you an advantage in the workforce. Studies have repeatedly shown that college graduates earn 50% – 75% more than high school graduates (Earn My Degree, 2010).

Now that you are here in college, your outlook on the world will start to change. You may already realize that you have opportunities limited only by your willingness to invest time and effort. On the other hand, you may have just started to realize that it is time to wake up and stop daydreaming. You have begun to take a realistic look at what you can and what you cannot do. Your potential career may no longer be based on what you always dreamed of doing, but is now based on a realistic assessment of what you can do. Whichever state you find yourself in, it is now time to move forward. This textbook has led you through this process of setting goals and making plans for college. Now you are poised to make some long term goals and expand your plans into the future.

Your expanded plans and goals will open your eyes to additional resources and assets, and may reveal unappreciated talents at your disposal. You will start to see yourself as a productive citizen in a global environment prepared to make a contribution to the world. You are an emerging leader. You have unique talents and expanded skills that are necessary to confront the challenges that you will face as you go out into the world. Understanding the challenges ahead of you will enable you to take a second look at your academic plan to make sure that you are developing the skills that you will need. Whatever the future holds, you will be prepared to take your place in society as an engaged, skilled, and educated citizen.

NETWORK BUSINESS SKILL
VALUES TARGET INTEREST
PLANNING ANALYSIS TEAM
MANAGEMENT TECHNOLOGY
SUPE SUCCESS VISIO
STRA GOAl
SOLUTION GROWTH SYNERG
RESEARCH INNOVATION DEAS
MARKETING EDUCATION ART
TECHNOLOGY TEAMWORK

It's a New World

You now look at college as a gateway into a new world: a world in which education provides not only new career opportunities, but also the opportunity to develop skills needed to take advantage of changing social contexts. When you first arrived at college, you brought a view that was rooted in your pre-college experience. There is nothing wrong with that. But now that you are discovering new opportunities, you may realize that college is preparing you for a world you may not have imagined.

In Units Two and Three, there was a lot of discussion about the diversity of college students in the United States. That diversity reflects the increasing diversity of the population of the United States. That increasing diversity is being driven by age. The median age of immigrant groups, Latinos, and African Americans is younger than the median age of non-Hispanic whites (Passel and Taylor, 2010). This predicts the future of an increasingly diverse work force. After all, younger people are more likely to have babies than older people.

The United States has a stable population. This is not true of other advanced economies, and that coupled with steady immigration of working-age people, will result in an international division in work forces by the middle of the Century. In the next 40 years, every other developed country in the world will experience a shrinking workforce while the US will experience an expansion. Current college students are at the beginning of this trend. All of this suggests that college educated people in the United States face both challenges and opportunities.

Table 4.1 Labor Force Growth (Schill, 2010)

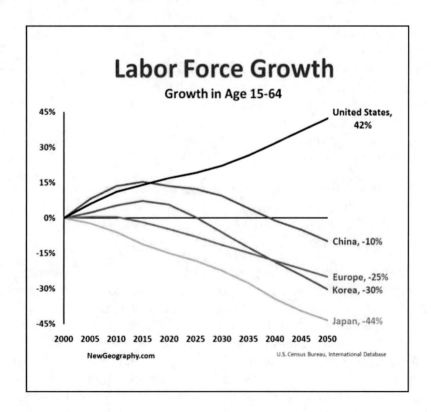

Leveraging Your Assets

If you have recognized the roots that have nurtured you thus far, and used them to branch out to new possibilities, you have learned to recognize opportunities presented by the diverse reality in which you are embedded. That reality reflects the future. Diversity is a unique advantage of a college education in the United States. Because of the international diversity of U.S. colleges, you probably have the chance to become a global learner simply by talking to people in your classes.

Most students can also afford to take advantage of other global learning opportunities, such as study abroad programs or international clubs on campus. That will provide extended opportunities to look at your place in the world. By doing so, you take control of preparing yourself as a leading member of a global workforce.

Because of the new emphasis on outcome assessment you have a unique opportunity to align your education and your interests. College accountability requirements, such as core competencies, allow you to constantly go back and make sure you are heading in the direction you want to go. They allow you to maximize your strengths and minimize your weaknesses. In the same way, you can develop skills that you will carry into the workforce. You already have some skills you can build on, but you will surely find you need to develop new skills. This discovery is the key to lifelong learning.

Student Voices: Renee

Renee never used her real name. She had never met an American who could pronounce it unless they also spoke her parents' native Laotian. She was born in the United States not long after her parents arrived as refugees, but Renee never really felt that she fit in. She had grown up translating for her parents, and there was a lot about U.S. culture that they did not understand or accept. Renee's parents encouraged her in school, but they always thought she would just go to college to learn to be a nurse. Renee was discovering, however, that college life offered much more than either she or they expected.

While attending a Student Resource day, Renee found there were a lot of ways for her to get more involved in college life. She took home brochures and flyers for several clubs and organizations. At first, Renee's parents did not understand the idea of a "club". Once they did understand, they thought she should join a health sciences club.

Renee was pulled in a different direction. She was intrigued by her conversation with the director of the Family Resources Center. All sorts of students got help from the Center. They shared their difficulties and funny stories about trying to find their own way in college. The director told Renee that sometimes other students from Laos came to the Center, and that Renee could really help those students. Renee was surprised when the director told her that a lot of American students also had difficulty adjusting to college life. It never occurred to Renee that Americans would feel overwhelmed by college. She thought that maybe she could help them, too. Renee's parents would still have preferred that Renee concentrate on nursing, but they liked the sound of the Family Resource Center.

Your Voice:

1. Why did Renee have a difficult time deciding which club to join?

2. What are some of the resources your college offers to allow students to safely explore new prospects?

3. What values do would want to honor as part of your involvement in college life?

College/Career Connection

Occupational Outlook

Once you complete your academic career you will begin your working career. What will the job opportunities be in your field once you graduate? Today's "hot job" may be cool by the time you graduate. What is the occupational outlook in your field, and will it still be strong when you graduate? Most importantly, what will be the new and emerging jobs in your field when you graduate? You may apply for a job when you graduate in a field that did not exist when you first started college.

These are serious questions to consider. The best way to tap into the future job market in your field is to explore the *Occupational Outlook Handbook* (Bureau of Labor Statistics, 2012). This site provides information on hundreds of jobs including projected growth rate, fastest growing new jobs, salaries, educational requirements, and job duties and descriptions. The 10-year projection of the fastest growing jobs can be a vital resource in your educational planning. The Bureau of Labor Statistics updates this handbook quarterly, and revises the entire handbook every other year.

Career Center

The career center on your campus should play a vital role as you consider your career options. It provides services to help you through the entire career planning process. Career centers typically offer assistance with:

- Career Counseling
- Career Resources
- Job Search
- Resume Writing
- Interview Assistance

Some students have never held a job and have no idea what they want to do as a career. Other students know exactly what they want to do and need help to do it. Some students may be returning to school after having been in the workforce for several years. Still other students may want to find a part-time job or internship. Regardless of which of those scenarios describes you, the professionals in your career center can help.

The first step in the career planning process, especially for students who have not yet declared their major, is to complete a career assessment.

Career assessment tools

It can be difficult to select the right career for you, something that meets your unique set of talents, interests, and skills. There are several career assessment tools that can assist you with this task:

1. Personality type and career planning assessments help you to match your personality type and possible careers.
2. Personal values and interests assessments look into your individual values and interests to lead you into careers that would be personally rewarding.

3. Career contacts and networks provide links to resources and industry contacts to help you to discover your ideal career.

Unfortunately, your preferred career may not have jobs that are in demand when you enter the job market. Career fields can become saturated, meaning that there are more people than jobs in a particular field.

A Forbes article by columnist Jenna Goudreau (2012) listed the 20 occupations in decline:

1. Farmers, Ranchers, and Other Agricultural Managers	11. Electrical and Electronic Equipment Assemblers
2. Postal Service Mail Sorters, Carriers and Clerks	12. File Clerks
3. Sewing Machine Operators	13. Prepress Technicians and Workers
4. Switchboard Operators	14. Computer Operators
5. Fast Food Cooks	15. Postmasters and Mail Superintendents
6. Agricultural Workers	16. Office Machine Operators
7. Data Entry Keyers	17. Pressers, Textile, Garment, and Related Materials
8. Word Processors and Typists	18. Florists
9. Door-to-Door Sales Workers and News and Street Vendors	19. Petroleum Pump System Operators, Refinery Operators, and Gaugers
10. Food Service Managers	20. Loan Interviewers and Clerks

This is not to say that you should abandon your desire to pursue a particular career field, but you should keep the current occupational outlook in mind as you progress through your degree program. You may find that you need to continue your education-transfer to a 4-year college from a community college, or pursue a master's degree following completion of your undergraduate degree.

The most important key is not to wait until you graduate to find out about the career opportunities in your chosen field. You will spend precious time, energy, and money on your college degree. You want to do your best to ensure you leave college prepared for a career that suits you and that has available jobs. Some students who receive degrees in shrinking job markets end up joining the dreaded ranks of the "unemployed college graduate".

Paying Student Loans

Another consideration is money. It always seems to come back to money. You will want to make the transition from starving college student to career professional. Of course, you want to be able to earn a living in your chosen field. You will also need to earn enough money to pay off any student loans that you may have incurred while earning your degree.

Let's look at a student loan repayment example:

Amount of loan (average student loan debt)	$25,250
Number of payments (10 year schedule)	120
Simple interest rate	6.8
Estimated monthly payment	**$287.70**
Total interest paid	$9,524.09

You would need a minimum salary of $43,155 to handle these payments along with other typical expenses (Ellis, B., 2011).

All this may seem overwhelming if you have not given some thought to your life after college. A successful transition from student to career professional requires you to look to your career future while you are still in school.

Student Voices: LaTonya

When LaTonya was struggling with an English paper she found help and support at the Academic Learning Center. She quickly built a rapport with her tutor who discovered LaTonya was an excellent math student. Even so, LaTonya was surprised when the director of the tutoring center asked her if she was interested in becoming a peer tutor in math. Because LaTonya had straight "A"s in all her math courses (something that she was really proud of), she met the qualifications and signed up to be a tutor for the next semester. She was careful to avoid interfering with her classes and the time that she would need to study to maintain her grades, so she did not schedule too many tutoring hours.

As LaTonya prepared for her next semester, she started to think about her options after graduation. She would graduate with an Associate in Science degree and thought that her job outlook was good, especially with her high grade point average.

She was also thinking about transferring to a 4-year college to pursue a bachelor's degree in science. She made an appointment with a career counselor to get more information and advice about which path to take. The career counselor gave LaTonya some good information about the current job market and her career options. LaTonya also talked to her older brother who said, "Get all the schooling you can while you can. I would love to go back to school, but who has the time with a family and a full-time job with regular overtime? If I had it to do all over again, I would get my education." This convinced LaTonya, and she began planning to transfer to a 4-year college after graduation.

Your voice:

What did LaTonya do to help her focus her academic future?

What are options that students have after graduation from your college?

What resources are available to you to help with your plans after graduation?

Expanding Opportunities: Transferring

By the time students have successfully completed one or two semesters of college, they begin to make adjustments to their objectives, goals, and behaviors. Some of these adjustments have to do with analyzing the skills they currently have and those they need to develop.

You may have learned that the school you are currently attending is not able to provide you with the degree or skills necessary for your career plan. You might believe that circumstances led you to the place where you are today, but in truth, you may have made little decisions along the way that culminated in your present situation.

Housman and Williams, in *College Transfer Success* (2012), offer a 5-step process for decision-making when transferring to a different college.

Step 1: **Choosing the Right Major for Your Career**

1. Self-Assessment

2. Choosing Your Major

Step 2: **Understanding College Culture and Your Personal Needs**

1. Researching Different Types of Colleges / Universities in the US

2. Exploring Your Individual College Needs

3. Investigating the Best Colleges for Your Career Choice and Major

4. Investigating Degree Requirements

5. Understanding Course Planning and Progression

Step 3:   **Researching Finance Options to Pay for Your Four-Year College**

   1. Exploring the Cost of College

   2. Investigating Different Sources Available to Pay for College

   3. Researching Ways to Save on College Cost

   4. Creating a Plan for Paying for College

Step 4:   **Creating a Personal Admissions Campaign**

   1. Researching the Admissions Requirements

   2. Conducting Information Interviews

   3. Understanding the Admissions Requirements

   4. Conducting College Interviews/ Campus Visits

   5. Creating an Admissions Tracking System and Timeline

   6. Completing Your Transfer and Financial Aid Applications

Step 5:   **Making Your Choice and Making the Transition**

   1. Evaluating Your Choices

   2. Identifying a Plan B

   3. Accepting your final offer

Housman and Williams suggest that your particular decision-making *process* is an integral aspect of making choices that lead you to ask the right questions that will lead you to a satisfying career (2012). How did you make your decisions? Use the chart below to look at the process you use to make decisions.

Recall a recent decision you made and mark the areas that you relied on in your decision making.

How I make Decisions:

My decision:	Gut reaction	Research	Friends	Family	Teachers	Skills	Other

Here are some questions you may want to ask yourself at this point:

1. What are the decisions you made that have affected your life the most?

2. How do you make decisions that affect your life?

3. Are you going to use that same process to decide your next move?

As they get closer to graduation, most students discover that they need to compile a resume or portfolio to represent their academic and work-related achievements. Knowing that interviews are in your near future, it is essential to take a good long look at what you are putting out there about yourself, and that includes your social media presence.

The Federal Equal Employment Laws prohibit employment discrimination against qualified individuals with disabilities, and prohibit bias based on race, color, religion, sex, or national origin, age, as well as other considerations. (Greenstein, 2010). Other information that you make available through social media may not enjoy those protections. This is a good time to take a look at what is out there on the internet about you. You may want to change the account settings on your Facebook page and check your other social media postings.

Nathan Newberger's article (2012) about interview skills gives great insight into what employers *are* looking for in potential employees. Organizational Skills, Critical Thinking Skills, Communication Skills, Interpersonal Skills, and Multi-Tasking Skills are important to land that great job. Some of these are known as transferable skills, but they are also called "soft" skills because they are not as obvious as a degree or certification.

Soft skills are learned, and anyone can develop soft skills if they are willing to take a good look at those skills they currently have and those they need to improve. The biggest enemy of improvement in these skills is the naive belief that they are not needed.

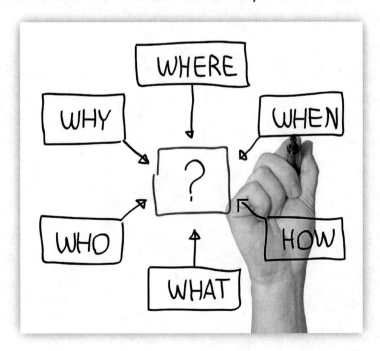

Student Voices: Carlos

Through conversations at school, Carlos was starting to get the big picture about work in the clinic. His demeanor changed as his perspective about his abilities aligned with an understanding about what it meant to be a healthcare professional.

Menial tasks like sweeping and taking out the trash had new meaning in light of the information Carlos was learning about the importance of hazardous waste removal in medical clinics. Trash removal became "hazardous waste disposal" that helped eliminate potential threats to people. The work became more important to Carlos.

Carlos was able to *project* a positive attitude because he *had* a positive attitude. His values and goals matched the work he was doing and the education he was receiving. He was involved in a profession that mattered to him, matched his goals and values, and helped others.

People noticed Carlos at work and commented about his value in the clinic. Students at school were attracted to his depth of knowledge and his positive attitude about the medical profession. They wanted to be in his study group. Instructors encouraged Carlos to continue his education and take advantage of opportunities that arose at the college to expand his network of colleagues.

When Carlos graduated from college, his network had grown to include professors, colleagues, student support staff, physicians and medical office personnel. He had a rich assembly of professionals from whom he could draw references for interviews, as well as a range of experiences that were unique and valuable.

Your Voice:

1. Why did the menial tasks in the clinic become important to Carlos?

2. How do our conversations affect the way we think about the skills we need?

3. How do you engage in your career conversation?

Taking a Second Look--Student Voices

Throughout this book, you have had the opportunity to meet five students as they discovered new insights and attitudes that allowed them to do what they really wanted to do.

In the Student Voices sections, LaTonya, Kyle, Tom, Renee and Carlos faced challenges. You identified those challenges, and applied your insights to them. In the following Student Voices, you will see that some of them modified their original academic paths. Others discovered whole new directions.

LaTonya: Mapping a New Course.

LaTonya's college career has been about self-discovery. She discovered her learning styles, improved study habits, resources for academic assistance, and an unrecognized interest in science. As her plans came together she decided to complete her associate's degree and transfer to a university. Her experience at the community college gave her the skills, resources and confidence she needed to discover new education and career goals.

What have you discovered about yourself as a student, and how will that discovery help you develop your goals?

Kyle: Taking a Second Look.

Kyle had to redefine his goals before he entered college. An injury sidelined his hopes for a career in professional sports. He discovered new goals, and learned how to use his college's resources to assist him in accomplishing those goals.

How have your goals changed since you started college?

Tom: Tasting New Options.

Tom realized that attitude played a role in the learning process. His public speaking class was a prime example of how having an open mind could lead to a whole new approach to his field of culinary arts.

How has your attitude about some of your classes affected your beliefs about college?

Renee: Reconciling Change and Tradition.

Renee came to college with her own beliefs and expectations, and discovered that getting a college education meant more than getting a college degree. She was able to reconcile new opportunities with her family's traditional values. She discovered that change did not mean giving up essential values.

As you reflect on your college goals, what adjustments have you made?

Carlos: Clearing Misconceptions.

Carlos learned the importance of not making assumptions about college processes and procedures. He also gained a new perspective that allowed him to see that seemingly trivial tasks were essential both in school and at work.

Describe a new perspective you have gained so far in your college career.

Where do I go from here?

On your journey to college student success, you have learned about yourself, your skills, your goals and the reasons you have chosen to pursue a college degree. You have learned about your college's resources and services, and how you can access and connect to them. You have even begun to acquire some of the skills needed to take the next steps on the journey to your career. Now that you have come this far, where do you go next?

This book proposes that college and career planning is a continually unfolding process. You have already identified opportunities your college experience offers. You can now map out the new insights you have developed.

You have come a long way and have become more aware of who you are and why you are in college. Taking time to revisit the steps you have already taken is a helpful step in the process for planning your next course of action.

As one former community college student shared, *"When I came to college, I knew what I wanted to do, but didn't know who I was. Now that I know a little about who I am, I'm not so certain about what I want to do. I know that whatever I decide to do, it will be okay because it will be something that fits with who I really am."*

The table below is a visual reminder of some of the considerations you have made during the process of discovering who you are and what you want to do.

Table 4.2 Where Do I Go From Here?

Once Again: It's About You

About you	You in college	Your future
decisions	college major	graduation
dreams	skills	transferring
goals	academic plan	career
	resources	networking
		goals

On the following pages, you will find some questions and checklists that will help you compile this discovery process in a summary about your achievements and goals. These resources can assist you as you track your progress from term to term and year to year.

Listed below are several questions about your college decisions, as well as a checklist of resources you may rely on to help you continue your plan for college success.

Once Again: It's About You in College

1. Three reasons I have decided to attend college are:

2. People and events influencing my decision to attend college include:

3. I degree I have chosen to pursue is:

4. The major I have chosen is:

5. If I am undecided, I will take the following steps toward choosing my major:

6. A SMART academic goal I have set for this semester or year is:

7. Important contacts I have made this semester include:

   Advisor:

   Career Counselor:

   Instructor:

8. My estimated transfer or graduation date from this college is:

9. My plans after graduating or transferring include the following:

Once Again: It's About Your College

College Resource	Campus Location	How I plan to use this
Tutoring		
Campus Security		
Counseling		
Registration		
Financial aid		
Library		
Career services		

About your future:

1. Three career planning resources I plan to investigate are:

2. Two careers which are a good fit for my chosen major are:

3. Options for service learning or internships related to my career include:

Success Checklist:

	I own or know how to access my college's catalog.
	I have scheduled meetings with my advisor or counselor.
	I understand the registration process at my college.
	I have a checklist of required courses for my degree.
	I have declared my major.
	I have researched several career options.
	I know what the career outlook is for my major.
	I know some people in my major.
	I have prepared a resume.
	I am connected with college resources like tutoring and student life.

Don't be discouraged if you find that progress toward your goal is not as swift as you had anticipated. The old saying "Rome wasn't built in a day." has been around for centuries because it is a good reminder that *accomplishments* take time. You have some ideas about the career you want to pursue. Ask people working in that field about the "swiftness" of their success. Most will tell you that while some rewards came early, their sense of achievement and accomplishment came more slowly. Hang in there. Success is worth the wait.

About the Authors

James A. Bazán, MA

James A. Bazán was a 32-year-old carpenter when he began college as a developmental math student at Indian River Community College in Florida. He graduated from IRCC with highest honors and went on to a bachelor's degree in journalism and a master's degree in sociology at the University of Florida. He also completed additional studies at the University of Florida.

He was the 2002 Instructor of the Year at Central Piedmont Community College, where he is currently a Sociology instructor. James Bazán discovered his love for Laura while working on the 1st edition of *College Student Success*, and they married two years later. This may be why he always lists *College Student Success* as one of his three favorite books. The Bazáns enjoy travel, and have participated in study abroad programs in Mexico and Costa Rica.

Laura L. Bazán, MS

Laura Bazán is Division Director for Collaborative Learning, English and Humanities at Central Piedmont Community College. As a graduate of Kent State University, Bazán began her career teaching high school deaf students in Kent, Ohio. After completing her master's degree in education from Queens College (now Queens University at Charlotte), Bazán became an ACA instructor at CPCC in 1997. She currently directs the academic divisions of ACA, English, Reading, Humanities, Journalism, Philosophy and Religion at CPCC which serve over 30,000 students annually.

In 2011 she received the Administrative Professional Award for Excellence at CPCC.

Linda J. Dunham, MPH

Linda J. Dunham is the Discipline Chair for ACA student success courses at Central Piedmont Community College in Charlotte, NC. Dunham has over 15 years of experience teaching ACA student success and study skills courses. In addition, she has extensive experience with curriculum development and faculty training in student success courses.

Dunham received her undergraduate degree in Spanish from Oswego State University in New York, and her master's degree in Public Health from the University of North Carolina at Chapel Hill. In 2010 she was the recipient of the Instructor of Excellence Award at CPCC, and was also selected as one of the top ten instructors in the state of North Carolina in 2011. These awards reflect her commitment to college student success. In addition to her role at the college, Dunham is happily married and is the mother of three daughters.

Elvira D. Johnson, MA

Elvira Johnson is the Coordinator for Learning Communities at Central Piedmont Community College. She is a graduate of Georgia Institute of Technology and has a master's degree in adult education from North Carolina Agricultural and Technological State University. She teaches several ACA courses, such as College Study Skills, Career Assessment, and College Student Success.

A longtime advocate of college orientation programs, Johnson helped develop this course and piloted it during the summer of 2003. She continues to promote college success by serving on the advisory boards of the Summer Bridge program, the Minority Male Mentoring program, and Service Learning.

References:

Amherst College Mission Statement (2012). https://www.amherst.edu/aboutamherst/mission

Arum, R. and Roksa, J. (2011) Academically Adrift: Limited Learning on College Campuses. Chicago: Ill. University of Chicago Press.

Atlanta Technical College Mission Statement (2012). /www.s125016.gridserver.com/about/history-mission-values.php

Alighieri, D. (2001-2012). BrainyQuote. Bookrags Media Network. www.brainyquote.com

Alda, A. (2001-2012). BrainyQuote. Bookrags Media Network. www.brainyquote.com

Allen, W. (2001-2012). BrainyQuote, Bookrags Media Network. www.brainyquote.com

Baker, N. (2001-2012). BrainyQuote. Bookrags Media Network. www.brainyquote.com

Baum, Sandy. (2011). Student Demographics. Chronicle of Higher Education 8/27/11, p 25-32

Business Dictionary Online (2012). Career. www.businessdictionary.com/definition/career.html

Business Dictionary Online (2012). Teamwork. www.businessdictionary.com/definition/teamwork.html

Campbell, Joseph. (1991). The Power of Myth. Anchor Books. New York..

Central Piedmont Community College (2012) The Basics. www.cpcc.edu/financial_aid/faq/basics

Central Piedmont Community College (2012). Budget - Cost of Attendance. www.cpcc.edu/financial_aid/faq/cost-of-attendance

Central Piedmont Community College Mission Statement (2012). www.cpcc.edu/administration/mission-and-vision-statement

College Board. (2012). Local Scholarships. professionals.collegeboard.com/guidance/financial-aid/local-scholarships

Cooley, M. (2001-2012). BrainyQuote. Bookrags Media Network. www.brainyquote.com

Covey, Stephen (2012). The Seven Habits of Highly Successful People. www.stephencovey.com/7habits/7habits-habit3.php

deSaint-Exupery, A. (2001-2012) Brainy Quote. Bookrags Media Network.
www.brainyquote.com

Disraeli, B. (2001-2012). BrainyQuote.Bookrags Media Network. www.brainyquote.com

Duda, Aisander. (2008). Still the People's Colleges: the Demographics of the N.C. Community
College System. North Carolina Insight. North Carolina Center for Public Policy
Research. www.nccppr.org/drupal/content/insightarticle/72/demographics-of-ncs-
community-colleges.

Duke University (2012) Academic Resource Center. web.duke.edu/arc/
Earn My Degree. (2010). Value of Education.
www.earnmydegree.com/online-education/learning-center/education-value.html

Ellis, B. (2011). Average Student Loan Debt Tops $25,000. CNN Money.
money.cnn.com/2011/11/03/pf/student_loan_debt/index.htm

Ellis, D. (2011). Becoming a Master Student. Boston, MA: Wadsworth Cengage Learning.

Federal Student Aid. (2012). www.federalstudentaid.ed.gov/scholarship

Fischer, Karin. (2009). Number of Foreign Students in U.S. Hit a New High Last Year.
Chronicle of Higher Education. Nov. 16, 2009.

French Proverb (2001-2012) Brainy Quote. Bookrags Media Network. www.brainyquote.com

Gordon, E. The Future of Jobs and Careers. (2009).
https://www.acteonline.org/uploadedFiles/Publications_and_E-Media/files/files-
techniques-2009/Theme_4(3).pdf

Goudreau, J. (2012) Jobs Outlook 2012: Careers Headed for the Dustbin. Forbes Magazine.
www.forbes.com/sites/jennagoudreau/2012/02/07/jobs-outlook-disappearing-dying-
careers-outsourced-eliminated/

Greenstein, H. (2010) www.inc.com/howard-greenstein/is-it-legal-to-use-social-network-data-
when-hiring.html

Gross Davis, B. (1993) Tools for Teaching. San Francisco, CA: Jossey-Bass.

Hart, Peter and Associates. (2006). How Should Colleges Prepare Students To Succeed In
Today's Global Economy? The Association Of American Colleges And Universities.
www.aacu.org/leap/documents/Re8097abcombined.pdf

Haywood Community College. 2012www.haywood.edu/vision_mission_and_goals

Housman and Williams. (2012). College Transfer Success. CPCC Press. Charlotte, NC.
Jobs, S., King, M., Jagger, M., Whitehorn, K., DiCaprio, L., Farrow, M. and Phoenix, R. (2001-
2012). BrainyQuote. Bookrags Media Network. www.brainyquote.com

Jordan, M. and Vancil, M. (1994). I Can't Accept Not Trying: Michael Jordan on the Pursuit of Excellence . Harper. San Francisco, CA.

King, S. (2001-2012). BrainyQuote. Bookrags Media Networkwww.brainyquote.com

Leonard, M. J. (2010). Major Decisions. dus.psu.edu/md/mdintro.htm

Lewis, H. (1997). The President and Fellows of Harvard College. www.harvard.edu/faqs/mission-statement

Li, Y., Whalley, J., Zhang, S., and Zhao, X. (2008). The Higher Educational Transformation of China and Its Global Implications. National Bureau of Economic Research Working Paper No. 13849. Cambridge: MA.

Mahfouz, N. (2001-2012). BrainyQuote. Bookrags Media Network. www.brainyquote.com

McKeachie (2011). McKeachie's Teaching Tips. Boston:MA. Houghton Mifflin Company.
McWilliams, P. (2001-2012). BrainyQuote. Bookrags Media Network. www.brainyquote.com

Migration Policy Institute. (2012). Foreign born as a percentage of the total US population. www.migrationinformation.org/datahub/charts/MPIDataHub-Number-Pct-FB-1850.xls.

Mullin, Christopher M. (2012). Why Access Matters: the Community College Student Body. American Association of Community Colleges. www.aacc.nche.edu/Publications/Briefs/Documents/PB_AccessMatters.pdf .

NAFSA. (2012). The Economic Benefits of International Education to the United States: A Statistical Analysis, 2010-2011. www.nafsa.org/publicpolicy/default.aspx?id=29416

Newberger, N. (2012). –www.worktree.com/newsletter/skills-to-convey-interview.html

NewGeography.com. .newgeography.com/content/001463-labor-force-growth-population-growth-age-15-64-2000-2050.

North Carolina Community College System (2008). A Matter of Facts. Raleigh, NC.
Pariser, Eli. (2011). The Filter Bubble: What the Internet is Hiding From You. Penguin Press. New York.

Passel, J.S. and Taylor, P. (2010). Unauthorized Immigrants and Their U.S. Born Children. Pew Hispanic Center. Washington DC.

Pew Research Center Publications. (2011). Is College Worth it? pewresearch.org/pubs/1993/survey-is-college-degree-worth-cost-debt-college-presidents-higher-education-system

Plato (2001-2012). BrainyQuote. Bookrags Media Network. www.brainyquote.com

Rogue Community College (2012) Transferable Skills Checklist. www.roguecc.edu/emp/Resources/transferable_skills_checklist.htm

Schill, Mark. (2010). Labor Force Growth, Population Growth Age 15 - 64, 2000-2050.

Southern University at Shreveport Mission Statement (2012).
web.susla.edu/Pages/MissionStatement.aspx

Statistical Abstract of the United States. (2012). Desired Outcomes of Education 1970-2010,
Table 286.

Tzu, L. (2001-2012) Brainy Quote. Bookrags Media Network. www.brainyquote.com

UCLA Higher Education Resource Institute. The American Freshman National Norms for Fall.

U. S. Bureau of Labor Statistics, (2010). Employment by industry, occupation, and percent
distribution, 2010 and projected 2020. Table 999100 Federal government, excluding
postal service. www.bls.gov/emp/ep_table_109.htm

U. S. Bureau of Labor Statistics. (2012). Occupational Outlook Handbook. www.bls.gov/ooh/

U.S. Census Bureau (2011). America's Family and Living Arrangements, Table MS-2.
Estimated Median Age at First Marriage, by Sex: 1890 to the Present.
www.census.gov/population/socdemo/hh-fam/ms2.xls1

U.S. Census Bureau. (2012). The American Community Survey. www.census.gov/acs/www/

U.S. Census Bureau. (2012). The American Community Survey. www.census.gov/acs/www/

U. S. Department of Defense. (2009) Active Duty Military Personnel Strengths by Regional
Area and by Country (309A)
siadapp.dmdc.osd.mil/personnel/MILITARY/history/hst0909.pdf

U. S. Department of Education. (2011). National Center for Education Statistics. Digest of
Education Statistics, 2010 (NCES 2011-015), Table 199.

U.S. Department of the Interior. (2000). Connecting Personality Types with Careers and
Jobs. permanent.access.gpo.gov/websites/doigov/www.doi.gov/octc/typescar.htm

University of Missouri – St. Louis, Admissions Office (2011). Changing College Careers.
www.career.missouri.edu

Yale College Mission Statement (2012). www.yalecollege.yale.edu/content/yale-college-
mission